W9-CDS-709

TEACHING
FOR
SELF-EDUCATION

TEACHING FOR SELF-EDUCATION

As a Life Goal

BY PAUL DOUGLASS

HARPER & BROTHERS · NEW YORK

TEACHING FOR SELF-EDUCATION

Printed in the United States of America

M-I

Library of Congress catalog card number: 60-5699

"Our opportunity as a nation is without precedent. We are called upon to produce on a clean soil an education that is sincere and sound, that values each differing mind, and with every encouragement, offers it advancement to the limit of its capacity, protecting it at the same time from illusion as to the true nature of its attainment and of what lies beyond. Upon such a foundation we may experiment indefinitely with democracy and be confident of the outcome."

William Learned

Contents

Foreword

William S. Learned served the Carnegie Foundation for the Advancement of Teaching as a staff officer from 1913 until his retirement in 1946. During the third of a century of his professional labor as the "Scholar of 522 Fifth Avenue," he participated in generously financed exploratory research as a member of the foundation's *Division of Educational Enquiry.* No matter what assignment commanded his attention, he persistently pursued his fundamental interest: the means of adjusting educational procedures and offerings to the ascertained abilities, interests, and needs of students as individuals. His purpose was to encourage a habit of self-education which would continue as an on-going intellectual activity throughout life. Learned's research was based on one dominating purpose: the improvement of *teaching for self-education as a life goal.*

Although the foundation in its obituary notice on the occasion of his sudden death on January 3, 1950, emphasized the fact that his reputation was most widely based on his work as founder and director of the *Graduate Record Examination,* his objective was to invigorate the functioning pattern of education. He foresaw the emergence of an era like the present, making demands for quantities of mature minds habituated to dealing with ideas through strenuous intellectual work. He felt that the stimulation of such a pattern was an obligation of the Carnegie staff, since the corporation's charter in particular commissioned it to encourage the discovery, formulation, and diffusion of true and useful ideas.

With time, space, and money to think, Learned operated as an authentic staff officer-at-large. He was particularly sensitive about his mission because he felt in a way that Carnegie had been responsible for the creation of much of the paraphernalia which, having outlived its usefulness, continues to encumber the campus. Of course he took pride in the foundation's initiative exercised in the early 1900's when the need for educational reform had been so urgent. For the last quarter century of his life, however, he devoted his mature energies to the definition of the outlines of an educational pattern which might prove in the last half of the twentieth century as radically wholesome as the foundation's work had actually been in its first half. In a valedictory statement issued shortly after the end of World War II, Learned observed that "education is craved like no other social provisions except peace." After a great social convulsion, he said, "there rises everywhere the major question: 'What is genuine education?' . . . Substitutes won't do."

As the years went by, Learned in his own meditations formulated pregnant models to demonstrate what he meant by "genuine education." He communicated these ideas in staccato insights printed in foundation reports. Thus his influence was assimilated into the bloodstream of higher education without a badge of identification or educational name plate!

Learned recognized a time at hand when higher education, confronted with overwhelming quantitative demands, faced a task that had "changed." He pointed out that the "change" lay in the direction of a clearer definition and pursuit of *intellectual value*. Long before the educational crisis which confronts the 1960's arrived, Learned pointed out that:

> Our opportunity as a nation is without precedent. We are called upon to produce on a clean soil an education that is sincere and sound, that values each differing mind, and with every honest encouragement, offers it advancement to the limit of its capacity, protecting it at the same time from illusion as to the true nature of its attainment and of what lies beyond. Upon such a foundation we may experiment indefinitely with democracy and be confident of its outcome. (1)

In a decade when the process of higher education is once again undergoing scrutiny, the thinking of William Learned lights a path and points a direction. His concepts had roots in enormous research and developed without scars implanted by competitive propagandas.

In this little volume I take as my task the discussion of those phases of William Learned's research and thinking which have theoretical and practical bearing on the study of the educational process which stands so high on the agenda of the 1960's. I have not undertaken to write a definitive biography of my good friend of other years, for he would wish none. I have attempted to bring into working focus certain of his ideas, the reconsideration of which may, I hope, have a wholesome and invigorating influence in educational discussions. My personal, intellectual, and professional regard for Learned and his educational realism of course is obvious throughout the book. It is precisely because of my conviction about the therapeutic usefulness of his ideas that I have taken the trouble to place his concepts in convenient form for general reading. For the most part the underlinings throughout the text are mine and serve to emphasize certain points for the convenience of the reader.

For their helpfulness in the preparation of this study, I express my thanks to Ben D. Wood, director of the Bureau of Collegiate Educational Research, Columbia College; G. V. Lannholm, director of *The Graduate Record Examinations,* Educational Testing Service, Princeton; Paul E. Elicker, executive secretary, National Association of Secondary-School Principals, Washington; David A. Jonah, librarian, Brown University, Providence; Eugene R. Smith, emeritus headmaster, Beaver Country Day School; Miss Florence Anderson, Carnegie Foundation for the Advancement of Teaching; and especially to Mrs. William S. Learned, New York. In a spirit of spicy helpfulness, she has provided documents heretofore unavailable. In her reading of the manuscript she has made spirited comments reminiscent of her husband who once observed that the polite name for "sentimentalism in education" that would confer rewards, advantages, or distinctions where they have not been earned is *"educational graft."* (2)

PAUL DOUGLASS

TEACHING FOR SELF-EDUCATION

1

THE EDUCATION OF AN ACADEMIC ICONOCLAST

A Man's Chance at Ideas

William S. Learned was born in Alpena, Michigan, on June 5, 1876. This county seat and flourishing harbor city, lying on both sides of the Thunder River on a small arm of Lake Huron's west shore called Thunder Bay, carried on considerable lake commerce in coal, lumber, limestone, and cement. Lumber and flour mills, tanning, veneer, and excelsior factories, commerical fisheries, and services supplying numerous hunting and fishing resorts in the neighborhood provided the economic lifeblood and defined the chief interests of the community. As far as the record shows, no experience in Learned's early life contributed to what became the central theses of his thought: (1) that *true intellectual goals should displace time-serving formulas in American higher education* and (2) that *the main stream of a student's learning should move in its own broadening channel*, independent of courses, of teachers, and of institutions. Nor did his undergraduate study in the Brown University of William H. P. Faunce or his graduate work in the Harvard of Charles W. Eliot awaken in his mind the germ of the idea for which throughout his lifetime he sought technical implementation, namely, that *liberal education is the satisfaction of a sound feeling for the relative values that permanently concern human life wherever they may be found.*

Up to the time of his study in Germany, Learned's education and academic experience followed the common pattern. He took his bachelor of arts degree from Brown University in 1897, taught at Cook Academy, Montour Falls, a village near Watkins Glen, New York (1897–1901), served three years as principal of University School, Providence (1901–1904), and spent five years as senior master of Moses Brown School also located in Providence (1904–1909). During the near decade of his career in the Rhode Island capital of politics, commercialism, and education, he performed his teaching assignments with conventional adequacy. With academic ambition propelling him to husband his time prudently, he took his master's degree in due course from Brown in 1908. Then, with what was at the end of the nineteenth century the educational objective of many a young American scholar of parts, he proceeded to Berlin and Leipzig (1909–1911) for continental study before going on to take his doctor's degree from Harvard in 1912 and serving there one year as research fellow (1912–1913).

Learned's teaching experience in three American academies provided the seedbed in which his educational explorations in Germany firmly rooted a concept of teaching *for* self-education. He began to envisage the genuine service of the true teacher as that of a *friendly critic, shedding light on a path toward a student's goal by providing for his work under a wholesome personal scrutiny.*

While he was studying in Berlin, the Carnegie Foundation for the Advancement of Teaching appointed him an exchange teacher assigned to the Prussian Ministry of Instruction (1909–1910). During the winter semester (October 1909–March 1910) he taught English to German boys enrolled in the *Oberrealschule Abteilung, Hohenzollernschule,* in Schöneberg, Berlin. He attended the teachers' monthly conferences; in prolonged daily contact he came to sense the real pulse of the instructors and the pupils. Wishing to see something of other institutions, Learned applied for permission and received a general pass to observe in all the elementary and secondary schools of Prussia. In the same way he obtained from the *Handels-Ministerium* the privilege of observing the *Fach* and *Fortsbildungsschule* in Berlin. Thus he was enabled to study with more or less thoroughness ten *Gymnasien* or *Oberrealschulen,* three *Fortbildungsschulen,* two

Fachschulen, and three *Volksschulen*. The striking fact which emerged from his observation was the thoroughgoing evenness and excellence of quality both of matter and of method in all Prussian schools of a given type. The conclusion had a directional influence on his later lines of inquiry. At the end of his appointment, Learned matriculated in the University of Leipzig.

In the tradition-rich Saxon city he wrote a perceptive report to the president of the foundation entitled *An American Teacher's Year in a Prussian Gymnasium*. (3) The document resulted in his employment by the foundation as a staff member—a lifelong relationship which continued from 1913 until his death at the age of seventy-three. In the writing of that first report Learned, as a young scholar of thirty-four, came pedagogically alive. For the rest of his life he searched with ample funds, philosophical insight, and mathematical measuring tools to identify the fundamentals of the process of higher education which he felt must hold true in all times and places, uncorrupted by momentary political, economic, and religious crusades which historically have sought to use the schools as vehicles of propaganda. He glimpsed a kind of system in which the *purpose of teaching would be to catalyze genuine self-education.* Such on-going purpose, he imagined, provides the kind of experience by which durable intellectual capital is created. Some thirty years later Learned tied the threads of his thinking together by asserting that "the most important key to the educational process is the fact that *emotional interest follows insight*, and that the interest which is aroused otherwise, unless it stimulates insight, gives little help to the sort of education with which the school should be concerned." (4)

The fundamental sociology of the Prussian educational system, it should be pointed out, did not appeal to Learned. The prevailing German idea of a teacher was that of drillmaster who inculcated a given body of knowledge into the mind of a preferably passive pupil. The ideal teacher stood as a master of his subject and an expert in its presentation; the ideal pupil as a completely receptive being. The system, which acted with military precision, was teacher-centered. It omitted no ritual which could assist in focusing the attention of pupils directly on the *Lehrer*. Nevertheless, the pupil, being always responsible for everything that went before, constantly reworked the field through various successive periods of his development to the mastery of his subject.

Despite the fact that he found too much brain and too little soul in the German school, Learned glimpsed a powerful educative factor in the ease and authority of instruction when *high and uniform standards are set by the examination for teachers.* He was impressed furthermore by one characteristic in the performance of the German students. Having no recourse to textbooks which "have it all in" and without the slightest inducement to "cramming," the German youth had every incentive to peg down ideas on the spot. Under such circumstances the teacher became a master of precise and effective presentation—a skill which the Prussians called *anschauliche Darstellung.* As a result of the method Learned came to believe that the German system kept a boy "in solution" throughout his course until the entire result was precipitated in a final examination. Monthly, quarterly, or yearly examinations had no place in the system. Learned thus came early to the conviction that "each student's self-education should constitute the controlling object of any educational agency that deals with him. *In order to endure, an education must be self-achieved.*" (5)

With his German experience behind him and his Harvard work completed, Learned moved to New York to begin his lifelong search to identify the tested fundamentals of *genuine on-going education.* Backed by the resources and influence of the Carnegie Foundation for the Advancement of Teaching, generously supplemented by grants from the Carnegie Corporation of New York, he sought to provide guidance for deepening the intellectual roots of American education by the development of scholars capable of the performance of *authentic and imaginative intellectual work.*

In the course of his studies Learned came to exalt the two basic notions of *discovery* and *cooperation* as the primary duties of the teacher. By "discovery" he meant, in the case of each student, what he can do. By "cooperation" he meant single-minded endeavor on the part of the teacher to assist the student in grasping ideas that are intrinsically important to him. He preached a realistic interpretation that would compel Americans first to interpret educational values solely in educational terms, and second to bring efforts into focus on the twofold process of understanding the student and of helping him to do his learning, not for credit, but for permanently outfitting himself in the direction of his best abilities.

Supported by research data, Learned proclaimed good news about education. In a word, he said this: "Give the American student a man's chance at ideas." Strip away "the paternalistic supervision that now chokes his interest and impedes his growth." Then the student's "morale in true intellectual activity will rise apace." (6)

How could the quality of such an educational performance be given direction to achieve fulfillment? Toward the formulation of an answer to this question Learned produced guiding evidence.

2

TOWARD PROFESSIONALISM

The Teacher, the Librarian, and the Student

Shortly after Learned began work at Carnegie, the Division of Education at Harvard University inaugurated a series of studies with the publication of his history of the German schoolmaster. Under the title *The Oberlehrer* (7) the volume traced the social and professional evolution of the teacher from his initial role in the church of the Middle Ages down to 1911 when Germans met in Steglitz to erect a monument at the home of Friedrich Paulsen to honor the educational historian and counselor of schoolmen. As Learned reviewed the development of teaching from its incidental position as a trade in the life of the priest to a collective awareness of mission in the nineteenth century, he rejoiced in the emergence of a professional spirit. This development, as he saw it, enabled teachers to state their aims, to undertake an exacting commission, and to become "the government's best counsellors and critics." (8) *In the writing of* The Oberlehrer *Learned identified the adequately prepared teacher as the sine qua non in the educational process.* The concept remained central in his thinking.

With his experience on the Continent fresh in his mind, Learned when he returned to America asserted the proposition:

> The greatest desire of every serious student of American education is to see the business of teaching American youth placed on an unquestioned professional basis. His vision is of a time when the teacher who shapes our careers shall be even more rigorously selected, more amply and purposefully trained, and more highly responsible for his performance than he who mends our bodies or untangles our personal relations. (9)

To understand Learned's subsequent thinking it is important for one to study *The Oberlehrer* carefully; from the very beginning he was concerned with the competent, imaginative teacher *and* with the trustworthy intellectual product of the educational process characterized by effective, cumulative thinking.

Professionalism among Teachers

In Germany Learned came to look upon the teaching force as the core of the educational system. In the peculiar character, training, and organization of the *Oberlehrer* he found a primary secret of educational excellence. In one of his first professional statements Learned took a clear stand for adequate and uniform preparation of the teacher. He wrote:

> Nothing . . . would so improve our conditions as this. Make his preparation purposeful instead of aimless, acknowledge and confirm his achievement by some competent and recognized authority and confine his instructions to those subjects which he is really prepared to teach. Instead of teachers by grace of a "general" college education, who dislike their work because they don't understand it and avoid their associates for fear of revealing their own incompetence, we could then hope for something of the German sureness of touch and the open fellowship of intellectual comrades. (10)

By an act of good fortune Learned presently found the opportunity to pursue the lines of thinking generated by his Prussian experience. Shortly after Harvard University Press published *The Oberlehrer*, Governor Elliott W. Major, of the state of Missouri, communicated an official request to the Carnegie Foundation, suggesting an inquiry to ascertain how the state might provide a supply of adequately trained and prepared teachers. In the areas of legal and medical education the foundation had already conducted definitive surveys and was giving serious consideration to proposals to undertake an inquiry into the preparation of teachers for American public schools which comprise the largest field of professional training.

Two weeks after the foundation acknowledged the governor's request, World War I broke out. Learned, assigned to direct the study, began work at a Jefferson City conference in November 1914; Carnegie issued the report early in 1920, months after the armed conflict had ceased. For more than five years Learned led task forces in the study of Missouri teacher education.

The report of the project was published in 1920 under the title *The Professional Preparation of Teachers for American Public Schools.* It became an epochal document in the history of education, establishing the need for a professional conception of ability, knowledge, and preparation as necessary equipment of teachers before the schools could become the effective agency in civilization which they aim to be. Speaking for the foundation Henry S. Pritchett summarized the message of the report by saying:

> The teacher must have before him a career that will attract the high-minded and ambitious student. He must be able to earn in that career a living salary and one that will provide for his comfort and for his protection in old age, but that is only one of the conditions to be fulfilled. Before all else we must have in our minds *a clear knowledge of what good teaching is,* of the methods by which teachers may be fitted for their calling, and under what supervision and organization the schools shall be conducted in order that the intellectual, social, and spiritual aspirations of teachers may be realized for the common good.
>
> Above and beyond all considerations of salary, it is necessary to have among teachers the spirit which rises out of professional training—adequate, scholarly, devoted—and which will make all who breathe its atmosphere proud to belong to a profession where such qualifications are widespread and recognized features. Without such a condition, no mere horizontal raise of salary will transform our schools into places of true instruction for children and for youth. (11)

Thus as his first important performance on the Carnegie staff Learned asserted the principle that "*education consists first of all in the superior quality and skill of its individual teachers, and is otherwise meaningless.*" (12) Indeed Learned believed that Plato's provision that the head of the state should be the director of education expressed "the unavoidable perspective in a completed democracy." (13) He applauded the state of Vermont for paying its commissioner of education more than any other state official, including the governor! In a classic paragraph Learned paid a high tribute to the teacher. He said:

If wars are to cease and democracy is permanently to hold the field, it will be a democracy with sufficient wisdom to confide this, its most responsible task, to its most competent citizens, and to prepare them thoroughly for its safe discharge. *Genuine education,* in a sense consistent with any honest vision of its meaning, *can proceed only thru immediate contact with keen minds fully informed and persuaded of what the rising generation may become, and dedicated to such achievement.* (14)

As Learned completed the Missouri study, Carnegie officials had been considering persistent applications for financial assistance from institutions of higher learning in the maritime provinces of Canada. With a view to developing a constructive policy for the treatment of the institutions that had applied for aid, Carnegie Corporation invited Learned to visit the provinces. In 1922 his report on *Education in the Maritime Provinces of Canada* was published. With educational statesmanship Learned pointed out that the one profitable policy for the people of the provinces was to shape the situation to provide university advantages of a first-class character for the residents of eastern Canada and Newfoundland. He found the most serious defect of education in the provinces, however, below the college level in the *primary need for well-trained teachers!*

Professionalism among Librarians

During the time that he was working on the Canadian study, Learned was loaned by the Carnegie Foundation for the Advancement of Teaching to the Carnegie Corporation of New York as an associate to Henry S. Pritchett, then serving as acting president of the corporation. While Learned was giving particular consideration to library problems, he drafted a private memorandum for office use summarizing the fruits of his research in the field. The document, expressing a personal point of view, was presently published by Harcourt, Brace and Company under the title

The American Public Library and the Diffusion of Knowledge. The volume brought a new perspective to library science. Learned set forth the concept of a functionally organized, professionally staffed, easily accessible, community-serving, culture-disseminating library operating as an active intelligence center through a competent staff of scholars trained in *fitting books to individual human needs.* He conceived of the free public library as a "genuine community university bringing intelligence systematically and persuasively to bear on . . . affairs . . . the chief instrument of our common intellectual and cultural progress." (15) Just as he had championed the professional education of teachers, so in this memorandum he emphasized the need for the provision of a sufficient number of thoroughly educated and technically trained library workers serving under conditions suitable for a permanent career. Learned felt that the 1,804 library buildings provided to communities in the United States and Canada by Andrew Carnegie at an expenditure of more than $43,000,000 expressed Carnegie's personal vision of the library as "a true community center for a comprehensive, popular education suited to all ages." (16) Learned had a profound respect for the self-education which Andrew Carnegie had given himself by the use of books. "Thus," Learned wrote of Carnegie, "with a book continually by him as he delivered messages, he matriculated in a university that he never afterwards abandoned." (17) With a phrase of Carlyle, often quoted by Andrew Carnegie, William Learned pegged down the idea that "*the true university of these days is a collection of books.*" (18) By 1924 Learned had placed himself amply on record: *two of the primary factors contributing to genuine education are first the adequately trained teacher professionally aware of his mission and second, the professionally administered collection of books adapted to individual concern, displayed to excite personal interest, and recommended to encourage growth.*

Professionalism among Students

Learned's concern for professionalism in teaching and professionalism in librarianship, in the middle 1920's, broadened into an inquiry into the character of the "professional" spirit among students. In the period of educational upsurge following World War I, the effort to open the doors of the secondary schools and colleges to all who desired to come tended to bring the ablest students to the same level of achievement as the poorest. Carnegie felt that the true interests of democracy were not being best served by an educational system which sacrificed the aspirations of the ablest pupils to those whose abilities were of mediocre quality. To explore the experience of England, France, and Germany, the foundation assigned Learned to a roving mission in Europe to ascertain how the three countries had succeeded in imparting to pupils an intellectual quality which combined a capacity for hard and consistent work with a pleasure and satisfaction in the pursuit. In preliminary discussions at 522 Fifth Avenue, staff officers came to the belief that "the quality of the educational process itself must be a large factor in determining the sincerity and the vigor of the intellectual life to which its students attain." (19) The foundation published Learned's report as *The Quality of the Educational Process in the United States and in Europe*. While this important study in comparative education concerned itself chiefly with the secondary school, it provided the springboard from which Learned moved into his significant studies of the relations of secondary and higher education in Pennsylvania. Learned began his monumental inquiry with a theory in his mind that "the knowledge that is power presupposes a mind actively at work and bent on the process of self-education." (20)

In his findings Learned minced no words. He said:

> What an intelligent father desires for his own son, an intelligent democracy desires and should provide for its children—*an education for each according to his capacity*. The conception of a democratic education as one leveled to a colorless mediocrity is as grotesque an interpretation of democratic principles as a state of health in which abounding vitality in those who can acquire it is deprecated on the ground that only average health is fair to the community. No one believes this nor considers it a sacrifice of democratic principles to

applaud supreme ability, whether it be in highly trained artists, in race-horses, or in baseball players. . . .

The foremost need of American secondary education is the frank establishment at the top of each considerable school system, of a school or a division that shall embody, for those capable of profiting by it, the best we know in the process of education for this period of life.

The main object of this departure from our customary practice is not to satisfy a few bright minds, still less to compete with European schools; it is chiefly to set up a scale of values in education that will bring order into our confused ideas as to what clear and serious thinking is and can do. (21)

Looking at American education in the perspective of his European experience Learned was impressed with how widely the intellectual operation of American secondary education differs from the wholesome atmosphere that surrounds school sports and games: student pursuits that are "honest, competitive, and thoroughly objective." (22) In a vivid paragraph he observed:

The boy who can jump over a bar five feet and six inches high bears an obvious relation to him who can jump but five feet four. The sports program involves throughout the selection and pitting of merit against merit in open, interesting struggle. Manage sports as we do our studies: minimize exact achievement, and measure a contestant by his "effort" not by his success; invite a pupil to compete chiefly "with himself"; make up teams alphabetically instead of by rigorous selection; keep chronic failures always on the squad; finally, to every one who can jump the bar at two feet give the same medal as mark of the finished athlete, and the significance and exhilaration that now attach to these exercises would rapidly ooze away. The frank objectivity that we put into sport, the European puts into headwork, and makes it engage the best powers of each pupil; we sentimentalize our education, and the youth properly finds his own inventions more important. . . .

We need a new scale of values not only for the sake of intellectual reality in the school but also for the sake of the community at large. If the whole nation is to attend the high school, there is the place to give each citizen a true vision of honest, objective human relationships. (23)

Learned identified *the demoralizing factor in American education as a misleading intellectual objective,* an objective, as he said, that

> is inherently irrelevant and that hampers rather than promotes his real educational development. *The active factor in a person's education depends on the nature of the intellectual problem that confronts him and the effect upon him of its progressive solution.* Instead of putting directly to the student the real problem that should engage him, the American school and college put foremost the mechanical task of taking sufficient hours of lecture or recitation to secure in four years the "credits" required for graduation. With a large number, probably with the great majority, of students the goal thus set up before their eyes obscures all other considerations; it offers a false objective to the weak and commercial-minded, and distorts the aim of those who are capable of better things; it substitutes for the idea of inner growth and enlightenment the notion of accumulating "points" that may be negotiated. (24)

With the publication of his report on comparative education, Learned was ripe to undertake the study of the relations of secondary and higher education in Pennsylvania. Out of this study were presently to evolve a philosophy and tools for implementing it which exist as permanent factors in American education. Learned had come to an awareness of the importance of the spirit of professionalism in the teacher, the librarian, and the student, all interrelated in the mutually sustaining interrelationships in the quality of the educational process, defined as effective, cumulative thinking.

3

THE MOMENTUM OF THE STUDENT

Accepted Responsibility for Self-Education

The image of the student which Learned came to entertain as a result of his studies was optimistic; some mistakenly thought it to be naïve and unrealistic. The cumulative body of statistical evidence developed in continuing Carnegie studies however verified for him this working hypothesis:

> Give a youth ideas that to him are big enough and important enough, and you can, with proper guidance, marshal behind them all the emotional resources and moral qualities of his nature. (25)

Learned liked to use a homely parable to emphasize his thesis that *no educational design can elevate intellectual performance above the level of the flow from a student's mind.* To supply the New Hampshire camp where he spent his summers, Learned drew his table water in demijohns from a pipe lying low over a trough. One day the idea occurred to him that he could plug up the stream and lead the water to the jugs through a hose, thus avoiding the considerable task of handling the awkward bottles. During vacation days he spent considerable time and ingenuity on a device for the purpose and applied it with confidence, only to find that nothing happened. In spite of a heavy flow at the lower level, nothing could induce a drop into his vessels. When, however, he exhausted the air in the hose, the water came to the top at once. A syphon eventually accomplished his purpose. Learned made the moral of the story explicit in these words:

I am not aware that even the canniest administrator has as yet devised a syphon that will permanently elevate the flow from students' minds. The utmost that he can do for the academic weakling is to exhaust the pressure of normal conditions and, by creating a vacuum, for one brief moment draw the level of apparent achievement up to the standard notches, only to see it fall back to its normal height the moment the unreal conditions and gratuitous concessions of school or college are removed. Meanwhile strong irregular jets of youthful power are spurting out under their own pressure from high sources all about, although for such needless overflow the administrative formula makes no provision. (26)

It was Learned's increasing conviction that a student's intellectual momentum can be generated by the application of four principles: (1) *sincerity and directness of aim,* (2) *thorough discovery,* (3) *cooperation toward the attainment of an individual and self-sought goal;* and (4) *honest objective appraisal of results.* Ben Wood remembers that Learned held the conviction that teachers should spend half their time ascertaining the abilities, interests, and needs of their students as individuals and the rest of their time helping students to meet their needs, exploit their abilities, and develop their interest to the optimum.

To Learned the student was no ordained receptacle for the two or three credit course the instructor is hired to teach. He saw little merit and much harm in administrative practices which intensify the struggle for term marks, quality points, standing on the dean's list, and so forth; all such devices falsely seek to elevate intellectual morale to an institutionally sponsored plane of social competition by the encouragement of credit hunting. Such goings on outraged Learned's concept of academic decency.

Learned liked to think of a curriculum as a mammoth reservoir of ordered and accessible knowledge, standing ready to be drawn upon by minds capable of grasping and interpreting its contents in books, laboratories, museums, and field resources. He explained his idea with this exhortation:

Fascinate young students with the real wonders of this paradise by direct contact, instead of presenting them with desiccated elements disguised under the appearance of so many term units or semester hours required to buy a degree, and one has taken the first and indispensable step in their education. Certain it is that an education will never be theirs until this illusion has been dissipated and they *learn to grapple for themselves with ideas in all their bewildering complexity, magnitude, and charm.* Moreover, it is precisely this that a goodly proportion of these young minds are eager to do. One awaits with few misgivings the daring college that will say to a group of capable beginners: "This institution with all its resources is yours, particularly the time of any and all of the faculty for advice and discussion. We make no requirements of you except that you remain four years, keep well, and behave yourself. But we shall expect to test and examine you frequently and in all fields in which you are likely to display growth, and we shall record with all possible accuracy the results of these measures or of any others that may reveal your actual knowledge and achievement in any direction. This is your opportunity and we are here to help you." (27)

Calendar exposure and time-serving formulas had no place in the educational thinking of William Learned. The American does not permit such measurements in any other aspect of his life "save in politics and in prisons," he observed, "where 'serving time' is normally equivalent to a promotion that is dangerously analogous." (28) He insisted that to be pointed in the right direction education at any level and for any purpose must discard the absurd assumption and apply the universal lesson of common sense, namely, that "*education is concerned with what one is, knows, or can do,* and when the material of education fails or ceases partly or wholly to function in one's mind or conduct, to that degree one fails or ceases to be educated." (29)

Learned's concern for the educational momentum of the student led him toward a concept of education which was delimited to an area of pure intellectual activity and increasingly to a content which was mathematically measurable. To him education signified simply "the mastery of certain sequences of important ideas to such a point that insights resulting therefrom shall be trustworthy and convincing to their possessor." (30) Learned's experimental findings dealt exclusively with the possession or acquisition of knowledge and some skills. He felt that the measurement of a student's knowledge and his powers of learning and retention provide the most definite essentials for establishing the quality status of any person's education. On the basis of twenty years of the study of certain aspects of the product and processes of secondary and higher education in America through the work of the Carnegie Foundation's Division of Educational Enquiry, Learned spelled out how students learn most effectively in view of their individual differences in the kind of educational environment which he envisaged. The twenty-two pages of his summary, published in the twenty-eighth annual report of the foundation, constitute one of the most important but overlooked road maps in the history of educational thinking. (31)

Learned started from the premise that for educational purposes *students in any classification are unlike.* From this proposition he derived two corollaries, namely (1) that *each student requires an adequate inventory of his existing equipment before his further education can be suitably planned* and (2) that *students, even of apparently similar attainment, should be treated with sufficient flexibility to insure for each the opportunity to satisfy the needs and manner of growth that are strictly personal to him.* Indeed from his research data Learned pointed out that in almost any large college population, whether freshman, sophomore, junior, or senior, students vary in their command of knowledge taught in schools, as well as in that absorbed from outside sources, from average tenth grade pupils to members of faculties at good colleges. Hence the college owes the obligation to every student it accepts to account for the working equipment he brings with him in terms it can understand and *will use* in directing his education. Learned declared the college

> should know in precise and useful terms the strength and edge of every tool of thought and expression [the student] possesses. It should discover the extent of his familiarity with all the important areas of knowledge. It should, in short, thoroughly map both the student's assets and his deficiencies, partly to make him realize that these exist, partly to fix the dimensions of its own opportunity or obligation. (32)

Even students of "apparently similar attainment should be treated with sufficient flexibility to insure for each the opportunity to satisfy the needs and manner of growth that are strictly personal to him. . . . Any mind requires a certain amount of free space." Just as the human body can not exercise when objects interfere and prevent its striking out," so a human mind is irked by restrictions that come too close. No amount of testing and classification can lessen the need for free and independent operation of the individual's own motives." Learned summarized the idea by saying that:

> In order to learn at all, each student must harmonize a team of variables peculiar to himself. Each starts with a different set of ideas and proceeds with a unique basic charge of emotional energy. Each "gets the point" or aim in view more or less clearly than his neighbor. Each has a different scale of values, is more or less suggestible, responds more or less to self-consciousness, and demands of himself greater or less thoroughness or finish from step to step. Each reacts differently to praise or blame or reward and diverts different amounts of attention to these considerations. Each applies the results of learning more or less widely than his neighbor, and deduces more or fewer significant conclusions. Thus each combination of these elements turns out a quite different product or produces a similar product in a quite different way. *To be a free mind and to learn profitably, one must at least be free to place the emphasis as one's aim requires, to grow according to one's nature, not according to artificial pressures that interfere.* (33)

The concern for individual differences had important consequences in Learned's program. For example, "no one would expect two individuals to gain from the same book the same impressions. No more can they reasonably derive from the same college 'course' the same results. In one case as in the other, an active mind requires, and in reality seizes, its own leeway to choose what it will ignore and what it will digest. Attainment should be judged not by paragraphs but as a whole, and on a scale far larger and of a different sort from that furnished by any 'course.'" However, he observed:

> Present practice inevitably produces "course standards" that seek minutely to mould performance to one blanket grade of A and imply that all who fall short are varyingly guilty. Such "marking" de-

feats its own purpose. It does not focus the student's emphasis on his own growth in either ideas or skills; it diverts his attention to the achievement of a composite "mark" the elements in which have clear meaning only to the individual who gives it—if indeed to him. The student's aim thus becomes spurious to the extent of his forced conformity to the alien requirement of the "mark." (34)

"Even a footrace provides a separate lane for each contestant," Learned said saltily. "The college can do as much." (35)

Continuing the figure of speech of track sport, Learned insisted that the college must define goals as clearly as the track coach and get the student's eye steadily fixed on them. In the hands of the college resides the obligation to "see to it that before each runner there lies an ample, unobstructed course whereon, without waste of time or effort, his full powers can operate to express whatever of worth there may be within him." (36)

But by what educational procedures could educational objectives be made as specific in the classroom as on the running track? Learned blocked out the general outline of the kind of educational program he felt the situation required.

First: *Specific knowledge and skills should be kept plainly before the student as his goals and should be dealt with realistically. To be effective such goals should be defined with a precision that can be understood, and, once reached, they should be recognized.*

Second: *Students of intellectual maturity suited to college study should be definitely expected to captain their own education. The college should show them how to do so, and should arrange its activities accordingly. The plan of campaign with its aims, its possible alternatives, extensions, and options should be fully mapped and comprehended in terms of ideas, not "courses."*

Third: *The essentials of education are two: understanding and skills. These universally diverse aspects of a complex mental condition should be sharply differentiated. Much of the waste of time and effort to be found in modern education arises from an attempt to combine the two in what appears like one operation.* (37)

Learned held that an institution that deals sincerely with a student will seek

to detach his notion of an education completely from that institution and from any other. Education is a body of personal understanding to which every experience contributes,—home, school, travel, but particularly the student's thinking as he reads and observes. Unless a person realizes this early and unmistakably, he misses the indispensable mainspring of all lasting education, which lies in the productive power of his own thinking on suitable material and apart from any intermediate agency whatever. (38)

Under present conditions the student

comes to revere the mechanics—the curricula, courses, credits, marks, diplomas—and the plaudits and prestige for having dealt skilfully with these irrelevant things. But he misses the central goal which is simply skill and habituation in recognizing, gathering, coordinating, and reflecting on significant knowledge from every source. In this the "C" man often outstrips the valedictorian. (39)

The knowledge and skills to be attained, so Learned held, ought to be mapped out by the college and explored by the student *far in advance,* not in terms of courses or books, "but in terms of *structures of ideas* that will always be valid and serviceable." (40) Said Learned:

These are the blueprints of intellectual construction from which the student's own world is rapidly being fashioned. They represent his connection with various aspects of life itself. They grow in volume and significance of detail as he proceeds to expand the limited college model into a permanent intellectual home and a career. There is nothing more entrancing for a student to brood over than such plans, if the college will but give him an intelligible and sympathetic start in their appreciation. (41)

Learned proposed to organize the static, uncoordinated segments of learning into something coherent and significant. He wanted to see ideas presented in dynamic fashion. His idea pointed toward *an entirely new type of college program and a radically altered program of communication with students.* He explained what he meant:

Students need prospectuses which, instead of vaguely listing fragmentary wares known only to professors, really illuminate for them the path of ideas through which one must move to become a historian, a mathematician, or a philosopher. As with the traveler abroad, the values gained are in proportion to one's sense of having been there before and of having known more or less in advance what was coming. To do this effectively for the several areas with which they deal, would be a faculty achievement of the first order. (42)

What Learned had in mind was a series of descriptive outlines of entire subjects, running from freshman to senior years. These outlines would deal with the subjects as they exist, not simply as they may be taught. They would indicate the limited portions to be discussed in the courses of a given year. There would be clear syllabi of other knowledge that might be expected to accumulate regardless of courses, in observant minds vigorously at work. There would be periodic, voluntary tests on important bibliographies assembled for particular topics. There would exist the privilege of examination in practically any field of application and of having one's achievement officially registered. Such features of a program, "if skilfully fostered with a little well-directed emulation, would emphasize the opportunity and, gradually, the obligation, not merely to learn a precise lesson in exchange for a 'credit' but to make continuous use of one's mind on matters worth while." (43)

In Learned's thought it was necessary to distinguish between what he identified as "understanding" and "skills." He explained the difference in this way:

Understanding requires curiosity, intelligence, and industry in putting questions and in getting them answered—all functions of a normal, self-educating mind. *Skill* is the power to use material thus acquired in various appropriate forms, constructing new sequences and contriving fresh applications of ideas. Skill depends on the constructive drive or originality of the individual, and profits much from the study and imitation of existing models and from the intensive criticism and suggestions of previously trained minds. It is the phase of education that pre-eminently requires guidance. (44)

Learned was careful to point out that, although understanding and skills are everywhere interlocked, the relationship is a one-way movement. "There can," he said, "be no skills without understanding, but understanding can be keenly appreciative with very little skill." (45) It was in the maturing of skills that Learned felt the students needed most guidance.

If the development of understanding and the mastery of skills constitute the two aspects of the task of the college, then the teacher must give attention to the method by which adequate and accurate knowledge is acquired. Learned asserted it as a principle that "*there is no way to ensure knowledge and understanding except to select the student who desires to learn and hold him responsible.*" (46) Although the intellectual undertaking is the student's own free responsibility, the college has the obligation to create a favorable environment, to supply the necessary tools, and to make personal explanation and orientation available at any point.

Learned inventoried what he conceived to be the four most important tools suitable for acquiring knowledge and understanding. He gave it as his opinion that some of these tools needed to be redesigned to perform their authentic academic function.

First in the resources of the college Learned named *books.* To him the library was the same kind of active intelligence center on the campus as it was in the community. The demonstration of Andrew Carnegie in self-education by the development of his power to get ideas from print remained a vivid object lesson in Learned's record; for it was in Pittsburgh in the year 1850 that Colonel James Anderson turned his library of four hundred volumes into a "Library Institute" for working boys and attended in person on Saturdays to exchange their books. *Books,* Learned stressed, *become a student's "chief intellectual tools for life."* (47) What Learned had to say about books and their use needs to be repeated:

> Most of the materials for an education are to be found in printed books. . . . Although the school has introduced him to them, the college must cement an intimate familiarity if not friendship. He must master their use in each of two important aspects: the single book and the book collection.

A student must know how to read. That is to say, before coming to college he should possess a considerable academic vocabulary, should be able to read rapidly and accurately, and should *like* to read. . . .

The college will probably have to teach the student how to read a book as distinguished, say, from a paragraph; that is, how to dissociate ideas from books and make them stand alone independently of print; how to read books and parts of books critically, without attributing to them undue authority, but using them as stocks of material facts and as contributing sources of ideas. . . .

A student must also be familiar with the mechanics and gadgets of a book collection. These are standard devices which require special habituation. They will forever be getting in his way or preclude the free use of the library entirely unless he discovers how useful they are in aiding him to find out quickly what he wants to know. . . .

Getting ideas from books is the characteristic foundation of an education. It is therefore the peculiar job of the student; one reads in order to understand. The quantitative measure of a student's work in college might far better be expressed by the number of hours per day that he reads rather than by the number of courses he takes. "I am *reading* six and one-half hours a day" signifies a fairly definite intake. "I am *carrying* fifteen semester hours" may, and often does, mean little except the *credits* which in one way or another are being engineered to a successful deposit. It is probably a fact that the college student will never settle down to self-directed, systematic, and discriminating reading and re-reading as *the chief means of his education* until he is rid of the course-credit system of compiling his virtues. The two do not go together. (48)

Second in the resources of the college Learned named *the course*. To Learned's way of thinking a course was a personally conducted book. The course, however, detaches ideas from books and gives them personal vitality; it should have no other object. To use a course for "credit" radically interferes with the "validity of the student's purpose and approach." (49) The main purpose of "a course," said Learned, "is to impart that understanding which comes largely through the spirit and attitude displayed in the explanations and *obiter dicta* of a wise teacher." (50)

Learned stated specifically what he conceived the nature of "a course" to be:

The method of the "course" is in general to effect understanding by means of orderly discussion, sometimes by exposition when the factor of interpretation weighs heavily. The business of the teacher is to make the matter clear in response to questions. . . .

The routine lecture of an earlier day, except on material not readily available otherwise or on matters of peculiar difficulty, is assumed to have disappeared. Formal "instruction" on the part of the teacher has vanished into books, in so far as understanding is concerned, or has given place to the various activities of the seminars in all that relates to the student's constructive exercises. This is not to suggest that we dispense with those finest hours of a college course when an unforgettable teacher has dealt profoundly with moving problems. It means only that time wasted and boredom generated in compulsory listening to fruitless talk is obviated, and that teaching be encouraged to stick to the point. . . . Good students fit to attend a course will not only ask intelligent questions; they will require intelligent answers. Herein lies the crux of the exercise: *the teacher must in reality teach*. . . . By and large, *the best criterion of good teaching* since teaching began *is the willing attention of able students.* (51)

Far from regarding "the course" as a permanently solidified item regularly recurring on an academic timetable, Learned looked upon it as a device for clarifying understanding of subject matter. Hence it should be set up informally as needed, should be treated as a good book would be treated—"the proper tool for the proper time and place." (52) Courses should be of any length to suit the purpose, "not padded out to a uniform cut to fit the space." (53) They should be open in whole or in part to any students reading in the given field who can profit by the discussion. Learned predicted the outcome:

By this means it should gradually become evident to the student that courses are intended to help clear up his knowledge and to project fresh extensions of it; not, as is largely true today, to guarantee its limits. (54)

In courses offered for credit, Learned saw a practice which perverted the student's motive in study and disintegrated the continuity in his learning. Pointing out that "courses for understanding are one thing; courses for credit are quite another," Learned presented a bill of indictments. Courses for credit:

1. Disturb and hamper the instructors.
2. Complicate administration with a meaningless and artificial system of bookkeeping.
3. Involve a mélange of marks for attendance, for knowledge-getting, and for constructive exercises.
4. Blur the specific aim in the student's mind.
5. Wreck all efforts at good curriculum construction.
6. Infest the relations of teachers with teachers, of departments with departments, of institutions with each other, "like an imperious demon."
7. Obstruct the real end in view.
8. Are responsible "for practically all the downright dishonesty in official collegiate procedure." (55)

As an alternative to the conventional course, Learned proposed a program which would focus the conscious effort of the student "on attaining a clear and permanent understanding of a certain area of knowledge for which he alone will be held responsible and over which no one of his teachers presides." Such a program would unite "student and teacher on a common footing and for a common purpose." (56)

Third in the resources of the college Learned named *laboratories, museums,* and *field work,* which parallel books and courses. These devices are instruments for obtaining deeper and more precise understanding.

Fourth in the resources of the college to encourage understanding Learned named *informal conversation.* He looked upon informal conversation, when well directed and congenial, as a mighty educational factor, a sort of universal lubricant which has "vastly to do both with intellectual understanding and with skills." He placed it beside the book, the course, and the laboratory. He stated the moving power of conversation in words that deserve to be read and reread:

Together with "the still air of delightful studies," conversation is an intangible of which the registrar takes no direct account. Its actual contribution depends altogether on the traditions and general atmosphere at the individual college. It may be enormous.

The bleak and threadbare conversation on some campuses reflects infallibly the meagre use made of books, the heavy preoccupation with "credit," the absence of "courses for understanding," the dedication of "bull sessions" to athletics and the opposite sex, and the unbridgeable gulf between faculty and students. . . . Ignorance that one might conceal from a teacher is confided to a friend—who may also prove to be a teacher. Things that really matter freely take first place, a characteristic that outweighs in its subtle influence almost any other factor one could name in choosing a college. A student dares be as good as he wants to be; and when this accompanies good-fellowship, no vista is more alluring.

Intimate use of books and close faculty relations help to generate this attitude, but at bottom it is a *function of the genuineness of the intellectual problem which the student himself faces.* An unrelieved "credit" system freezes it. (57)

It will be recalled that Learned drew a sharp distinction between "understanding" and "skills." He held that *skill in using ideas should be the main concern of an educational institution.* Knowledge-getting should be largely turned over to the student, while the *pressures and critical energies of teachers should be concentrated on constructive exercises that will most surely develop specific powers.* It was precisely at this point that Learned became most radical in the primary sense of the word, which means proceeding from the root. "The tools of knowledge and understanding have so increased on all sides for anyone who can read," Learned said, "that it is foolish longer to keep an expensive organization merely to say over what is printed and check its repetition." (58) Be done with this inherited pattern! The time has arrived to test the good faith of the student by putting responsibility for knowledge chiefly on him. Modern examinations can tell at once and accurately when he knows enough. Provide the best facilities for learning that are available, yes, but "*concentrate the efforts of the college on those things a student can not do for himself and in which good criticism and advice are indispensable.*" (59) Here a field of service lies open to the college where it can perform superlatively well. Relieve the college of the job of policing knowledge! Allow it to educate students who wish to learn so that its groups of educated teachers can perform a telling and congenial service.

But how? *Before a teacher can help him, a student must be in a constructive situation.* His response is likely to be most sensitive when he is engaged in original exercises and in activities where his own creations are laid open to view. At such a point good teaching has its most profound effect. Seminars, disputations, practicums, laboratory work—these are some of the terms used for exercises intended to develop or test the student's constructive abilities. They should be set up for as many types of intellectual training as the college deems profitable or can afford. Naturally they will differ in each field and they should and could easily differ according to the particular outlook and equipment of each student.

> A term paper with topics more or less alike, when assigned to a class of sixty men, furnishes an admirable comparative basis for solving the teacher's problem of awarding three semester hours of "credit." That is likely to be the chief reason why it is given, at least in that form. But there will be some for whom the performance is a needlessly bad prescription and many for whom it is a bore. Its very uniformity gives it away. Were it not for the "credit," each student might be dealt with much more satisfactorily. (60)

Learned lumped all such exercises which represent the student's own reaction to knowledge under the inclusive category of *seminars.* He felt that "seminars" broadly defined *should constitute the backbone of a student's formal knowledge.* In contrast to "courses" which the student should use as he uses books, taking few or many and moving in or out at will, *his seminars should be few in number and carefully tailored to his needs.* Admission to various levels should obviously depend on his knowledge tests. Into these seminar engagements the student must "put his back." He would have no choice but to carry through. This requirement might vary from a freshman book report or biographical essay to a serious assignment involving the critical study on the spot of the current budget in a large city.

"You do not give a student A's and B's for this sort of thing," Learned pointed out.

> You watch him work, observe what and how he does, the abilities he shows and where he fails; you note outstanding traits and the effect of conscious efforts to alter or develop them; you observe his influence on others and that of various outside forces on him. You compare doubtful conclusions regarding him with those arrived at by other teachers. All this finds its way into a summary record and is added to the student's history to supplement his knowledge inventories.
>
> Thus the student is variously tried out in the effective use of ideas both oral and written, and is systematically judged by what he can produce—by the best he can produce with all the resources he possesses and under the most favorable circumstances. His background, the other fields from which he draws, and even his wider knowledge of the field concerned—such factors as these are clearly indicated by his test inventories recorded from time to time elsewhere, and always available to his counsellors and teachers as to himself. *This differentiated procedure, aimed first at knowledge, and then separately at power,* at least ensures that faculty and partial measures of a student's knowledge shall not be confused with hasty judgments as to his power in the attempt to find a single numerical equivalent that will satisfy the registrar for each four months' stretch of attendance. (61)

Obviously any such concept as this compels the rethinking of the meaning of the so-called curriculum; Learned believed that "a curriculum *is nothing more or less than the actual sequence of mental acquisitions of a given mind as it makes its way through the world of ideas by which it is surrounded.*" (62) The curriculum is comprised of substantial clusters of related ideas sharing a general unity and capable, in combination with other such clusters, of building up a higher unity. The ideas are stated in progressive sequence in order to introduce the student to organized thought about man and his environment, by guiding his reading, and by developing a coherent philosophy. "A curriculum presented to the student as a series of courses is ineffective." (63)

Since every mind behaves in a different manner, every curriculum is necessarily different. "Believers in the efficacy of a fixed curriculum of 'courses' corresponding to a catalogue announcement," Learned pointed out from his records

> have only to examine the tested outcome. They will find that while, in one case, a course "takes" far beyond its intended scope, in another it will leave no durable trace; while one student devours the books laid out and asks for more, another's mind is being filled with wholly uncatalogued stuff. The test records produced by identical course lists taken by any two persons reveal results that are identical only in their unvariable unlikeness, frequently in extreme degree. A student who can read rapidly and grasp ideas quickly may satisfy the equivalent of three curriculums in the time that a student for whom books are difficult worries through a part of one. All this may occur while each student in these pairs received "credit" for the same group of "courses." (64)

Learned considered it to be axiomatic that if it is an ultimate equipment of definite ideas we are after, we must state clearly what these are. He proposed that:

> We must give up trying to construct compulsory channels out of "courses" which, we assert, will lead the student to his destination. When he has no clear conception of what his destination is to be, he can have no power to recognize it, should he happen to arrive. Such walls and fences do not hold, nor do the paths they indicate suit the varying motives, speeds, or imaginative powers of the students they aim to serve. The college senior is bewildered because he can form no just estimate of what he has got in comparison with what he set out to get, and he realizes at last that he never knew what it was that he set out to get. (65)

Learned wanted students with their preceptors to be "pioneers in goal-making" for the kind of academic explorations necessary to undergird the kind of program he envisaged. Suppose, he said, that certain minds are inspired by the aim to understand a selected period of culture as reflected in its origin, its history, its literature, and its philosophy! "Credit" courses cannot be made to fit such a purpose.

They are too cumbersome; built for convenient interchange with other institutions, they are like apparatus packed and crated for shipment and taking up several times the necessary space. Without the padding, their parts might fit well as essential aspects of a unified purpose, but in their present administrative shape they are wasteful and unmanageable. Any student might rightfully ask: Why know nothing about physics, or psychology, or American history because you can not devote the time to take a "course" in each? (66)

Learned wanted comprehensive curriculums to state in as related detail as convenient the "goals of knowledge to be comprehended as large units and tested as such, instead of as term 'courses' to be formally *absolved* for 'credits.'" (67) Such comprehensive curriculums, he asserted, would furnish a flexible invitation suited to the varying needs and ambitions of each student.

The man of single-track mind may content himself with a minimum of general information, or may burrow exclusively in the field he prefers. The philosopher, on the contrary, believes that no aspect of human thought or achievement is alien to his need. He finds that with diligent study he is competent to seize the emotional outcomes in many different fields and fit them into his total picture. The all-important thing, however, is that both philosopher and specialist should realize, as clearly as a common-sense description can make it possible, what it is that he is passing over and what it is that he is determined to possess. (68)

Thus, the very nature of curriculum statement as carefully explained to a student in advance may, if well supported in practice, have much to do with a solution of the *liberal* versus *vocational* questions facing his choices.

For a choice there is bound to be. Whatever official prescriptions may demand, the elements that live, that enter permanently into the student's equipment and determine his eventual career are going to be those that are personally congenial and stimulating, those which at the time satisfy his own philosophy of life. *It is for the college, therefore, through its advance descriptive blueprints of the curriculum, so to scrutinize and publicize to the student the values latent in every field as to stir interest, excite intellectual ambition, and arouse the student's determination not to leave so fruitful an area untouched.* (69)

Learned came close to academic heresy when he took the position that a liberal education is not necessarily the study of art, literature, philosophy, or any other subject in particular. A liberal education is rather

the satisfaction of a sound feeling for the relative values that permanently concern human life wherever they may be found. *Humani nihil a me alienum puto* is still a good motto for the liberal mind. Philosophical appreciation of values is not dependent on mastery of detail. A student with a competent discipline in one area possesses a pattern of thoroughness in any other, and no field of human interest may be excluded from his horizon. *It is this wholeness of life as well as its depth at certain points that the college should emphasize and by suggestion seek to realize in the student's mind.* (70)

Learned's proposal to present the educational values of the curriculum to the student in groups of related ideas, rather than in existing "credit" lengths like stove wood, had for its purpose their reintegration on the logical lines of the student's own intellectual requirements. Such integration he held is indispensable to the student's efficient education.

William Learned believed that growth in education is

comparable with natural growth; it must have continuity; it must have nourishment and exercise from within; especially, it must have time. It is profoundly affected by the clarity and emotional interest with which its ultimate aims are defined, held, and extended. With favorable conditions, results mature simply through staying by the same main line of ideas long enough to see them in many relationships and to become acutely aware of their nature. The fragmentation of the curriculum under the current course-credit system is due, plainly, to the interruption of responsible continuity of thinking that occurs with each completed "credit."

Learned said:

It is like snipping off a plant after each month of growth. Were real responsibility maintained and made inherent in the situation by discarding the paralyzing virus of "credit," many bad features of college courses would soon disappear, and they would come to serve their only function—*an aid to understanding where understanding is needed.* The "credit" stifles all practical impulse to review, and review is the healthy student's breath of life. The chief cause of his present intellectual sloppiness and confusion is his pose of thinker with material that he has read hastily but once, has not pondered, and has never clearly understood. (71)

Learned found an important corollary of continuity to be staying by an important group of ideas until comprehension has matured. This he found exemplified in the reading habits of certain individuals and the reading requirements of certain institutions. Some books, he observed, can be

adequately read by scanning the table of contents, the page heads, and the conclusion; some deal with ideas so intimately that a careful reading, marking, and re-reading of marked passages is needed; a number of the very greatest books need to be re-read deliberately many times at such intervals as will permit the intervening growth of the individual to re-interpret the book. As for education in most matters contained in books, its quality and range can be judged with fair accuracy by the number of times the student has re-read certain volumes. Few college students know this, chiefly because their institutions have never told them. Indeed, it would be very difficult, if not impossible, for an institution to explain this effectively to students and at the same time justify a system of course "credits." (72)

One administrative procedure essential to make possible the kind of college Learned hoped to see develop lay in the *evaluation of achievement.* It was upon the development of measuring tools for the evaluation of achievement that Learned came to concentrate his efforts. This program was to him his avenue of maximum strategy; the tools it provided were necessary to achieve the kind of intellectual objective he felt desirable. He saw in the development of modern, objective examinations a convenient and relatively trustworthy instrument wherewith to measure *one* factor in education that is highly important and that can be isolated from all others with comparative ease. That is *"the element of knowledge irrespective of any use thereof which the student may be capable of making."*(73)

The essential requirements of sound evaluation, as Learned saw them, were (1) that the achievement recognized be comparable and accepted coin of the intellectual world, and (2) that it be as specific in denomination as its character will permit. The measured performance provides advantages.

> The knowledge and understanding that a person acquires are the factors in his education that are most completely under his own control. They may be increased at will by thoughtful reading and observation, even without formal schooling, depending on the individual's intelligence and industry. Consequently, although knowledge and understanding are indispensable conditions for higher educational processes, they are bound to be exceedingly variable in scope and quality. A good measure of knowledge therefore makes it possible to adjust minds to that form of activity from which they can derive the largest benefit and to ensure that the education they possess is a genuine and not a fictitious quantity. (74)

The measured results have particular value to graduate schools for they gauge the scope and accuracy of the student's present knowledge, a factor vital for further study which the college record covers very imperfectly or not at all. Further, instruments of the kind Learned believed in and developed provide a basis for measuring knowledge independent of the individual college attended. The practice of inviting collaborators from many colleges to construct and criticize the tests effectively eliminates the peculiarities of any single institution; the knowledge structures on which such tests are based are naturally valid anywhere; the pattern follows no course or curriculum divisions. Such examinations are "inappropriate" said Learned, "only where students are 'credit'-bound and are measured solely by what they have 'covered' of a partial or an eccentric selection of material." (75) Further, the comparable scales in such tests are fixed by hundreds and thousands of students from many colleges.

> Thus the student is protected from a "mark" given on a single teacher's estimate of success with an arbitrary selection of subject matter—a mark which, as an index of his knowledge of the subject, may be quite false, although he may have been led to think otherwise.

In short, his knowledge is appraised in terms of standard coin, understood and respected. (76)

The objective measuring tools however constitute only one device of evaluation. Learned did not propose that the record examinations should be the sole and only measure of performance. Quite the contrary was the case. Side by side with the measurement of knowledge he placed the necessity for provision of appraising power.

Since "education for skill and power is the chief function of every teacher and of every faculty as a team, so *the efficient appraisal of skill inevitably becomes a central concern in every good teacher's thinking.*" (77) In contrast with the measurement of knowledge however, the just appraisal of power is an undefined and unorganized task. Power and skill, as Learned understood them, are the concentrated business of seminars, laboratories, and similar constructive exercises. Of course knowledge and understanding go hand in hand with constructive effort, but they may easily be *prerequisite qualifications.* In any case, as necessary, they may be easily predetermined by tests. Learned felt that the appraisal of power should be specific. He said:

> The first requisite . . . is an accepted and convincing definition by the faculty, of what constitutes the characteristic abilities and skills in a given area—mathematics, literature, etc.,—which are to be the goals of a student's constructive effort in that area. Apart from mere understanding of the book, just what are the qualities that original work in mathematics should reveal or develop? Is it speed and accuracy of analysis? Is it resourcefulness in applying a wide range of mathematical tools? Is it sheer persistence with difficult problems? Is it an esthetic flair for neat and "elegant" logic in the solution? Furthermore, are the desired outcomes agreed upon by all the mathematics teachers in the college? Are the evidences of such outcomes understood in a common terminology? In other words, will the statement of a student's ability in mathematics depend solely on the peculiarities of the teacher or teachers whose seminars he happens to take, or will he be given a pooled and verified judgment on substantial evidence according to carefully prepared and accepted standards? (78)

But measurement of knowledge and understanding and appraisal of power and skill to Learned comprised only the raw data by which the distinct educational problem of a final evaluation for each individual could be arrived at. Said Learned:

If institutional education is to justify the confidence we place in intellectual development and in the outlook resulting from individual effort with ideas, we shall be compelled to *lift the final conclusion regarding it from the domain of the adding machine to the level of critical judgment.* From the moment when each teacher, according to his conscience or his convenience, tries variously to weigh his single term "mark"—this fraction for attendance, another fraction for quizzes, a third for required reading, and the remainder for a term essay—no human being, under the course-credit regime, interferes with the automatic mathematical play of the factors so contributed. No one takes the liberty of an expert glance at the student to see what has become of him. The average which governs his diploma may be that of a brilliant beginner who has quite petered out, or of a mind that has found firm footing after desperate struggles. What should be said of this as the supreme culmination of our educational logic and insight? (79)

Learned felt that the generally current practice stultified the entire educational performance. At this point he expressed his profoundest distress; in acid words he pointed out:

We assume to possess the intelligence to create an elaborate mechanism for a certain difficult purpose. But we then refuse to look the product of this mechanism in the face and to require that same intelligence to shoulder the responsibility for what has, or has not been, accomplished. *Our fear of self-criticism has obliged us to wait for the shock of a social upheaval in which only realities can save us, in order to get the evidence clearly in view.* (80)

To Learned the most sacred obligation confronting a faculty lies in the final evaluation of a student's educational attainment. In its adequate discharge a staff of teachers, he felt, will

accumulate more wisdom as to the precise nature of the process before them than in any other aspect of the undertaking. The available aids, such as test scores, are important and should certainly be included as showing the scope of a student's equipment or lack of equipment in all significant fields, and in pointing up comparisons with appropriate names. (81)

But for Learned, precise mathematical statistician that he was, the core of the matter lay elsewhere. He was convinced that

nothing can take the place of a considered, carefully confirmed and worded estimate of a board of experienced teachers, in view of all the evidence. This should contain no meaningless phrases. It should describe as exactly as possible in educational terms the demonstrated abilities of the student, where they lie and of what nature they are. His limitations and their compensations, if any, should be clearly set forth. Marked gains or changes over the entire curriculum period should be pointed out. Clear evidence of special powers as seen by the mature observer should be emphasized. Honors ratings or classification should be equally specific in their scope of reference. Such a document should present *the mirrored image of the student in regard to defined educable traits which the faculty considers important and should be intelligible both to the student and to any competent inquirer.* (82)

When an academic description of the student in such terms is written out in a skillful way, Learned foresaw that the report would prove of greatest value to the students and afford the college at least the satisfaction of a task completed in the terms and spirit in which it was undertaken.

Underlying Learned's concepts lay the changed structure and quality of society.

The acceleration of modern communication has not only brought distant places near, it has telescoped the individual's personal education by flooding him, whether he will or no, with important notions both *viva voce* and in print. What schools and colleges once taught with deliberate and impressive step, today, "everybody knows." The task of education, it seems, is no longer to instruct *de novo,* but to correct and straighten out ideas, to select from the welter that assails every eye and ear those conceptions that are fundamental, and to see that when the student emerges such concepts are matured and understood. This done, its further and most difficult obligation is to ensure that wisdom so furnished shall be able to wield its power of leadership with effect. (83)

Learned modestly assumed that his blueprint of a pattern of higher education suitable to the age contained proposals of well-known practices, long since tried out in various institutions that have successfully attacked the problem. Their chief virtue, "if virtue they possess," he said, "resides in their emphasis on the "inherent simplicity, responsibility, and directness of the education process as opposed to the accretions of an exuberant institutionalism that has served its day and lost its essential face." (84)

4
ADMISSION TO COLLEGE

Continuous Intellectual Voyage and Present Worth

While probably the final institutional obligation of a college lies in the evaluation of the intellectual achievement of the students it graduates, the lines of development begin to take shape with admission. Hence Learned turned his research eye to a study of entrance policies and programs.

As a point of departure he asserted that both in the mind of the candidate and in the popular estimate the one visible turning point in an American youth's educational career which outranks all others is *admission to college.* As Learned stated it, admission to college

> puts the seal of seriousness on his cultural aspirations, or at least fixes the social atmosphere in which he hopes to move. Graduation, advanced degrees, practice of learned professions—all lie in a straight path beyond this parting of the ways. The best that inspires a thoughtful child's personal dream, or the desires of parents who are ambitious for him in a social or intellectual direction, are bound up with "getting into college." (85)

It bothered Learned to see that the movement from secondary school to college was unaccompanied by an alluring intellectual purpose. "The sole object of the pupil is to 'get in,' and that of the school is to 'get him in,' to the exclusion of any emphatic and engrossing educational idea," he said.

> Each activity is measured mainly by its effect in surmounting this artificial barrier rather than in laying a real foundation of knowledge

consistent with an educational purpose, already clearly understood, in which the college is to supplement the school. (86)

Exaggerated emphasis on the overt act of admission raises three problems. *First,* educational values which should be uppermost in the student's mind recede in importance before the pressure of admission technique. *Second,* "the individual and his unique educational make-up, instead of constituting the focus of attention in shaping for him a suitable and continuous personal program from below upwards, are lost in a maze of fixed option-patterns mechanically handed down from above, with innumerable internal weightings that invite the manipulation which now ensues." (87) *Third,* the freshman, after prolonged and violent effort to be admitted, finds himself engaged in exactly the same work as before.

He is committed to no new purpose and follows no new procedure. His altered surroundings interest and impose upon him, but otherwise he might as well be enjoying promotion from one year to another in the school from which he came. (88)

For both the "teacher-wise" student who looks upon college as a "finishing experience" as well as the purposeful, serious student, admission to college is, as Learned saw it,

a sort of spasm, ill-timed and needless. It greatly disturbs the preceding years, but is meaningless educationally and answers no fundamental questions. It is a concession to institutionalism—important to the prestige of a pedigreed Alma Mater, but wasteful and misleading for the student. (89)

Learned held it to be fundamental that the only suitable data for the college to consider in projecting the education of a person beyond the limits of the school is (1) the evidence of a deliberate acquaintance with the pupil and (2) a cumulative appraisal. Only such information is helpful in furthering education which, as Learned said, "is a gradual and complicated process of displaying both trustworthy constants and fluctuating variables." (90)

Learned analyzed the two prevailing methods of transfer from secondary school to college, namely, *examination and certification based on the school record.* He felt that no satisfactory solution of the admission problem can easily be conceived that does not do full justice to each of the two principles which divergent emphasis in a twofold practice has thus far thrown into apparent opposition.

In admission to college by certification Learned identified serious difficulties. The student's secondary school record as submitted presents a series of "scattered and hermetically sealed courses," characterized for the most part by a minimum inducement to genuine thinking apart from teacher, text, and credit. Given the unintegrated secondary curriculum and its disorganizing effect on the pupil's mental equipment, a college, after a study of the transcript, said Learned, is "almost as much in the dark as to the quality of the pupil's present working outfit" as before. (91) Further, the ratings by certification are subjective in character, the measure having been taken by the teacher privately and arbitrarily of a relatively small group of the teacher's own pupils. The teacher rates them on the way he thinks they have responded in the performance of tasks which he himself has chosen, assigned, and administered. "Knowledge of the subject, experience with pupils, opportunity to judge, health, personal likes and dislikes, school promotion policies—all count as concealed variables in the teacher's verdict." (92)

But what of admission by examination which, together with certification, might provide a standard for admission? The real question to be determined is this: What does the pupil actually bring with him? Granted that the mere ticking off of the units in a curriculum affords no assurance that a mind has generated important thoughts of its own or has the means wherewith to do so, yet adequate diagnosis is not as simple as the alternative to certification might imply. Learned was leery of what he labeled "snapshot" judgments. Knowledge, he warned, is subject to enormous fluctuations between the momentary maximum achievable by intense concentration for purposes of final examination and *"the normal unforced level of retention and use which is the sole true index of fitness to continue."* (93) Learned distrusted any academic performance which could be described as an artificial routine, "the conscious filling of the reservoir in order on a given date to produce the highest possible pressure of a peculiar and limited sort." (94)

Present Worth

On the basis of his studies of the relationship of secondary to higher education, Learned formulated the fundamental question: "What are the principles on which a satisfactory and trustworthy transfer from school to college can be effectuated?" (95) To the answer of this question he devoted enormous thought.

He began the formulation of his solution by pointing out that the school is the nursery in which the future college student, like the future stenographer, mechanic, or salesman must be grown and studied. Under suitable conditions and with competent scrutiny Learned was sure that "the genuine student announces himself at once and unerringly." The task of the college "is to ensure that his subsequent learning and training flow naturally and with certainty out of this indisputable, and essentially determining, period of his growth." (96)

From such a premise it follows, "as the night follows day" that a true chart and record of the pupil's school activities is second in importance only to the activities themselves. Such a chart becomes the chief reliance of any admissions procedure that is based on defensible educational ground.

It is precisely at this point that certification performs its chief collateral function. It shows over as wide a range as possible the sort of ideas with which the pupil is most successful, the kind of thinking that commands his personal momentum and initiative, the skills in which he is poor as well as those in which he is conspicuous. Learned elaborated:

> All this comes into play not merely to "get the pupil in," but primarily to determine what sort of college, if any, what phase of further study, what vocational or avocational ends, may wisely be proposed and advised. And the record, if understood, immediately becomes of quite as much importance to the college as to the school itself. It is their joint agreement on its interpretation and the appropri-

ateness of the particular offering the college has to present, *in view of the record,* that justify it as an educational instrument. (97)

Side by side with the utilization of such a true educational record in the admission process Learned placed pupil analysis in terms of what he called "*present worth.*" By "present worth" Learned meant a cumulative analysis or summary, as complete as possible, of the pupil's intellectual, emotional, and physical equipment and competence at a given moment, including his entire past and unlimited by his particular activities. Away with the naïve view of education as a state that arises automatically solely from having "taken" a great variety of short courses for each of which one has received a credit! "No other country tolerates the conception in this crude form," Learned observed. In fact, to be pointed in the right direction, education at any level and for any purpose must discard such an absurd assumption and apply the universal lesson of common sense, namely, that "*education is concerned with what one is, knows, or can do, and when the material of education fails or ceases partly or wholly to function in one's mind or conduct, to that degree one fails or ceases to be educated.*" (98)

Learned held a college examination program to be defective when it is satisfied with only a final cross section of the pupil's mind—"one for which violent and distorting preparations are made, resulting in a picture that leaves many important things about the candidate unsaid, and in which most of the things that are said are, to some degree, wrong." (99) He felt that he saw an obvious remedy, namely, to push the demand and inspiration for "present worth" back to the beginning of formal education and incorporate it as an educational attitude throughout the entire educational practice. He put the idea in these words:

What we need, in order to guide these children, is a series of truthful pictures, in as close succession as possible, that will reveal the normal, unforced, and significant action and tendency of their minds and which, in its totality, will admit of but one interpretation. Without the pressure and extraneous incentive incident to the present final examination, we should ascertain, step by step, what sort of ideas pupils welcome, assimilate, and grow on, and how these are related to the enormous reservoir of knowledge that is available. Little by little, the pupil as well as the teacher would acquire the salutary attitude that *it is what one becomes, what one really knows, and what one can surely do that count in education, and nothing else whatever. Anything at this level of development that has the effect of substituting an outward sign or value for the grace of permanent inward change and gain,* as is notoriously true of high school "credits," *should arouse the implacable aversion of every teacher.*" (100)

With such an attitude toward the pupil and his work, Learned felt that *the entire secondary course would itself become a systematic and critical study of the individual.* Thus, years before the actual transfer to college took place, the pupil's record would disclose far more about his fitness for college than any entrance examination now reveals. *The student would eventually come to college—not as a problem in admission,* for this matter would have been settled long before—*but solely as a problem in placement,* both in kind of work and in degree of advancement. And even these points might well have been settled earlier as to his true intellectual status on the basis of knowledge secured and made available by his school.

Learned predicted that the attempt, by means of the extended and adequate record, to show the gradual development of a pupil's "*present worth*" would have a far-reaching effect even with such a curriculum as that to which most of them now submit. He explained:

The proposal to ignore the convenient stratification of learning that has become familiar, to stop judging pupils by what they seem to know of material just studied, and to recognize rather at each comprehensive probe, from term to term, simply what we find and *all* that we find, would at once set up a healthy ferment in any curriculum. Should a pupil normally display growth from one semester to the next in command of his knowledge of science as a whole, even though he may be studying but one branch of science? Ought knowledge in the entire field of history and social studies to stand still, or go back, simply because the pupil happens to be earning his "points" in some other department? Is it good sense to pass over without recognition all the extra school experience of a pupil where independent thinking can most easily be stimulated? Traditional attitudes on these matters receive a powerful jolt the moment we give a pupil, by means of interesting and cumulative tests, often repeated, the slightest reason to put genuine and increasing purpose into both school and private study, or to resurrect and discover new meanings and fresh applications in ideas that he had supposed, being "credited," were therefore dead. (101)

While an academically satisfactory and clerically simple cumulative form to move with the student on his continuous academic voyage did not develop as Learned had anticipated, the present discussion attempts to divorce the mechanical problem of a workable form from the substance of the educational idea which Learned wanted it to incorporate. In his dreaming Learned assumed the development of an adequate cumulative record substantially as comprehensive as he felt desirable. He pointed out that in lieu of such a program, the admissions stipulation of even the best colleges still dominates the process and governs the program of tests to be given or the special qualities to be watched for in certain promising pupils.

The "ivied" admissions strait jacket was repulsive to Learned; his research convinced him that a college rarely or never defines its goals for the choice of students at the time of their admission or before! During the first year or so of college a kind of sorting and sifting process goes on. In this process the secondary school record plays an "ignominious role." Hence any expert and revealing study of the pupil beginning, say in the sixth or seventh grade, finds its curve extinguished after the twelfth grade under the grinding pressures of arbitrary demands behind which lies merely the groping for a generalized and nebulous academic excellence.

Briefly put, Learned said that what he was proposing was a true inventory, progressively maintained, of a pupil's initial equipment in terms of a cumulative series of measures capable of giving, at each point, regardless of what the pupil may have had or when he may have had it, *an accurate index of the levels and scope of his normal working knowledge.* In the Pennsylvania studies supported by the foundation Learned gave attention to the details and use of the kind of "progressive inventory" of which he felt the need. In actual practice, however, the model which Learned and his staff devised, replete with scales and detail, required more clerical work than schools with limited secretarial assistance were able to carry on. While Learned's too-complicated cumulative record forms influenced schools not having some kind of cumulative record system, his format did not catch fire.

While Learned was probing into the need, a committee of the National Association of Secondary-School Principals itself developed a cumulative form which came to be widely used. Larger schools, further, began to develop their own forms. The association on its part developed standardized secondary-school record and personality forms, conceived of not as "cumulative" as Learned understood the word, but rather as "transmittal forms." The form now most generally in use was developed by the association and issued upon the recommendation of a joint committee on school-college relations of the association and the American Association of Collegiate Registrars and Admission Officers.

According to Learned's view, the perspective appropriate to the secondary school is the entire span of the pupil's intrinsic education, not "an arbitrary path to the college gate—a path to which the pupil is more or less forcibly adjusted and which disappears entirely after he enters." (102) Learned emphasized his point:

> If the educational process is at any time to center in the pupil rather than in the institution, it must do so here, and if it is to do so with effect, the lines discernible in a young pupil's interests and powers must radiate directly to possible ultimate satisfactions that are genuine and not be deflected midway by an interruption like "getting into college"—an interruption that stimulates many alien interests and that fails to coordinate and classify his thinking along the main line. (103)

Learned felt that the more completely education concentrates on the pupil, the more precisely it learns the pupil's real abilities and powers, the more urgent becomes the need for sharper definition on the part of the college, not of entrance requirements, but of *what its own various offerings mean, and what they demand,* in order that the essential choices and opportunities open to the pupil may be understood. The college needs information, not in terms of units or semester hours, but in accurate terms of knowledge, kinds and tendencies of skills, extent and character of minimum limitations. Schools sending pupils to specific colleges should have intimate and authoritative knowledge as to what sort of minds ought to choose what kinds of subjects, what background of knowledge is desirable for success, to what sort of activities they lead. Learned put it like this:

Pupils of acute mentality and scholarly promise . . . deserve to be confronted early with the genuine terms and conditions governing these momentous choices, while the rigmarole of "getting into college" is pushed into the background. We deplore the wasteful "day-to-dayness" with which secondary pupils commonly proceed on their intellectual rounds, and forget that it is not their fault. They can do no other, save when, from their parents or from a casual teacher, they are so fortunate as to catch the enduring vision of what they unwittingly seek, and would at once recognize if it were presented. Obsessed with institutional emphasis, our forms encourage this shortsightedness and will continue to do so, so long as "getting into college" is the theme instead of preparation for whatever, in the college, best suits a long and true view of the pupil's education. (104)

Learned sympathized with the feeling that a great part of the weakness of American secondary education is due to the fact that "it is always interrupted in the middle of its job." (105) He explained what he meant by saying that wherever, in spite of college requirements, the secondary school succeeds in working out a true formula for a child and gets him happily under way, the college steps in with a different set of values and, ignoring the findings of the school, tries to conform him to its plan. Thus there follows "a clash of two successive authorities, friendly enough but almost wholly ignorant of each other, that in the interests of a harmonious and consistent education should, at *all costs,* be reconciled." (106)

The Comprehensive Cumulative Record

It has already been noted that the comprehensive cumulative record, as Learned conceived it, failed to achieve any measure of permanent acceptance. Because of the importance of the concept in Learned's model of an educational program, however, it is important to discuss the idea more fully. Learned wanted a record which both parties could trust and *use.* He felt that this educational tool was of first importance and maximum strategy. In addition to recording measured performance, ranging over the entire field of organized knowledge to establish present worth, Learned proposed to add year by year the concrete observations of teachers—the *same* teachers who follow through and who define the pupil's behavior in successive situations and with different kinds of academic material. Thus, perhaps more than a year before he was graduated the pupil would be able to identify and select the *one* college out of the many best suited to him.

If such a usable record were available, it is clear that admission requirements would recede in importance. The college would understand the student in view of the powers he showed as his work had been observed and tested. The college could read and understand the record of this work *in the same sense* in which the school read and understood it. It could develop from the record the normal, understandable performance of a candidate for admission in terms that it could compare accurately not only with others of the same age and grade, but also with the average of its own advanced students. If two units of elementary Latin and a half-unit of ancient history failed to appear, that was the school's lookout in doing for the boy what, in its judgment, was best for his welfare.

Learned took issue with the selective tradition of some institutions which keep their admission lists undetermined as long as possible, welcoming transfers and late comers to the competition, and thus keeping all candidates uncertain of their fate until the last moment. Such policy, said Learned, *is bad educationally both for the pupil and for the school that prepares him.* No attitude could more emphatically glorify the mere "getting into college" at the expense of a well-defined long-cherished intellectual purpose in process of steady and satisfactory fulfillment. Learned felt it of immense importance to pave the way for students who, as pupils, have early shown conviction as to what they are about, who consider, plan, and work at their own studies with discriminating feeling for the serious values ahead, both in school and college, rather than to assemble a group who can "get in" brilliantly, often for the very reason that they have never been diverted by tenacious intellectual interests that are genuinely their own, and for whom "getting by" is thereafter the natural sequel.

What Learned was after was to make the school's horizon coincident with that of the college just as that of the parent in the earliest years is coincident with both school and college. The successive designers and artificers of a young person's education ought to work together on the same pattern without essentially disturbing it. The kind of record he proposed, Learned felt, would enable the college to cooperate with the school by accepting provisionally, years in advance, pupils whose minds are already dealing with education rather than with institutions. Then the eventual transfer from the one institution to the other becomes little more than a geographical incident. When properly used, *the record was thus to serve as both chart and compass.*

Learned recognized that his proposal departed from the kind of policy historically supported by the foundation. The foundation had laid great emphasis on the suitable preparation of students accepted by institutions on its associated list. In the schools whence these students came, the greatest confusion prevailed. There were no accepted units of measurement for work completed. One of the first notable services of the foundation, not only to its member colleges but to the country at large, was a general conference of the officers of the organization with representatives of the National Conference Committee on Standards of Colleges and Secondary Schools and other well-known educators. Out of the conference came the definition of the so-called rigid time units that have since prevailed in the administration of American secondary education. While in its day the device represented a distinct advance and performed an indispensable function in aligning the school forces of the country in what was as near a common understanding as, under the circumstances, could then be achieved, Learned was frank to say that none recognized more clearly than the foundation that *these standards had served their purpose.* With changed conditions and better tools such norms became obsolete. They should give place to more flexible, more individual, more exact, and more revealing standards of performance as rapidly as these may be achieved. Into the confused process of "getting into college" Learned thus injected two new concepts: *continuous intellectual voyage and present worth.* Central in the continuum of intellectual growth would then stand the individual and not the institution.

Learned would have viewed with interest the development by the Educational Testing Service of the evaluation instrument described by the long title of *School and College Ability Test and the Sequential Tests of Educational Progress,* referred to by the alphabetical letters as S.C.A.T.–S.T.E.P. Four years in the making, this "family" of tests came at a time when American education was under attack by the press and being seriously studied by public and educators alike. In announcing the publication of the test, the Educational Testing Service said:

> Our problem as educators is not, as many of those outside the field have claimed, how to educate our young people like their Soviet counterparts, but how to maintain education for the *individual* in a democratic society in the face of today's enormous physical and financial burdens on the schools. (107)

The S.C.A.T.–S.T.E.P. was described as "the first yardstick of achievement" that can be applied from the fourth grade through the second year of college.

To explain the usefulness of the tests, the Educational Testing Service spoke much in the language of Learned as follows:

> First, in the strongest educational tradition, it enables you to measure the ability of a student to *apply* the knowledge he had gained to new situations. You test not simply for factual recall, but for skill in using information acquired.

And second, you measure the individual's capacity to undertake the next higher grade level—a comparison of achievement with the student's own ability to achieve.

Learned would have rejoiced in this development; but he would have regretted that it required the ascent of the Sputniks and the contests of the cold war to produce it. Rather, Learned would have felt that such an instrument derived its justification from the school's paramount obligation: "of unlocking and plumbing the capacities of its students, one by one, for mastering ideas to the point of grasping their essential relations." (108) In the refinement of such tools of measurement Learned saw the opportunity to end the "hocus-pocus" of time-serving formulas. He expressed his vision in the Inglis Lecture (1932) when he said:

> The school and college of the future will possess and use every possible aid in objective measurement precisely as the physicist depends upon his gauges, scales, and meters. We shall find too, as does the physicist, that a profitable study of the imponderables that evade us, first becomes possible when we learn to observe them in the presence of factors that we can measurably understand. (109)

5

THE COLLEGE AND THE FRESHMAN

Preceptorial Semester

In the course of the Pennsylvania study Learned identified for especial attention two particular problems. The *first* centered around "the complete absence of a competent and responsible personal guide in the delicate business for which a student comes to college." (110) The *second* stemmed from the fact that "the modern college either has not learned how or has not thought it worth while to point out convincingly to the new student what, as a whole, education for him may mean." (111) He addressed himself to these two subjects. Out of his concern there emerged the idea which he called the "preceptorial semester." Learned held the college directly accountable for its failure to anchor the freshman's attention firmly at once to the main task at hand and to create for the new student a true perspective from the strange and varied elements of his new life.

Learned reviewed the kaleidoscopic experiences of a new student embarking upon the serious matter of his education: (1) a hurried interview with a dean, a dean's assistant, or a dean's adviser; (2) a patient waiting in a registrar's line to dispose of the formalities of registration; (3) the onsurge of the campus mass—the vivid interests of fraternity life, sports, class politics, campus society, and personal diversions. At the very time when the freshman most needs an anchor, he is adrift!

To reconcile these warring claims upon the "pliable and wavering newcomer, to protect or at least to hold him in college," said

Learned, "'personnel work' has arisen." He found to his disappointment that this service had been directed

> to smoothing out personal difficulties, to scrutinizing physical and mental health, and to facilitating social contacts and enjoyment so that a student will "do his work."

By "doing his work" Learned felt the college referred to fitting the student into the complicated machinery of the campus. He reported that nowhere had the personnel program been concerned with "ensuring that a student will understand his real business of *systematic and profitable thinking.*" While the personnel service hedged a student about with excellent advice on how to get through college, it did not profess to "teach him the use of the compass whereby he may steer his own way to an education." Learned deplored the fact that he found so little evidence of well-defined intellectual aims resulting from clear knowledge. At least, he observed with his dry humor, the secondary school can hold up the aim of "getting into college"; the college for its part, however, encourages the hope of "staying in long enough to get out according to a time and credit formula." Lacking valid aims, the freshman's thought, he admonished, is led to the end of the first semester. There both teacher and student are halted until the latter is prepared to suggest what he for various reasons proposes next to elect. "And so on," said Learned, "through four years." (112)

> Thinking at long range and on a large scale with accumulating material and momentum becomes, therefore, a mere accident instead of conscious habituation as the central feature inherent in the college situation. It is as a chance by-product, if at all, that one comes upon what should be the most satisfying rewards of systematic study. The college curriculum is amazingly like the disarticulated skeletons of curious fish or certain small mammals that one sees mounted on panels in museums. Between each two whitened bones appears a narrow segment of black cloth. Form and outline of the whole structure are perfect; but there are no muscles, no blood vessels, and no nerves—nothing to enable the ensemble to function as a unit with force and purpose. The situation as to courses within the college curriculum is identical, except as the individual voluntarily displays initiative and

modifies it for himself. The only possible unifying element from course to course in a college curriculum is *close reading and persistent thinking* on related materials; this, owing to our reverence for "courses" and our installment system of accumulating college credit, is the one thing that is not required. Thus, there are great opportunities at present untouched for intellectual orientation in the major outcomes of college work, as well as for fundamental exercises in the nature and method of education. All of this could be profitably discussed with freshmen and, if well done, would perform excellent service in convincing a student that *what he consciously does in college with his mind is paramount.* (113)

What practical solution did Learned propose to resolve these problems? *Begin with the freshman at the beginning of his first semester*, he advised. Provide for contact with good teachers at the outset of a student's college career. He argued that if graduate students with habits of thinking definitely formed and ideals fully developed derive their major inspiration from the weekly conference with the chief teachers in their fields and depend heavily upon them for direction, the freshman, entering with good intellectual habits scarcely established, with many bad ones well started, and with mind bewildered, has desperate need of such conference!

William Learned spelled out his idea for a preceptorial semester for freshmen by laying down this rule: "*No student should be admitted to the campus who cannot be placed immediately in charge of a competent representative of the college who will make him a subject of deliberate study and will personally direct his education.*" (114)

Learned wanted to eliminate from the campus vocabulary the word "adviser" with all its accumulated connotations. He wanted to dissociate the function from its label. As understood at present, according to Learned, the work of the adviser is both casual and indefinite. In the advisory relation, initiative and responsibility usually rest with the student. Hence contacts develop a peculiarly fragile nexus and often never occur at all. In cases where contact is established, the content of the relation often, on the adviser's part, is a friendly but irresponsible interest, and for the student, at best a repository for personal confidences not to be overdone lest student opinion frown on him for "boot licking." Learned asserted that the personal bond between the college and the student it proposes to educate should be of a radically different nature. Friendly interviews with dean or president are all very well, he said, but the college that

> proposes to secure and hold the serious intellectual attention of a student should demand it *from the outset* in the most emphatic fashion by means of forceful, personal contact, sufficiently prolonged to fix the pitch that it is desired to maintain. For this an "adviser" will not do; it requires a relation that *expresses substantially in itself the purpose of the college,* and *it must be completely integrated with college procedure.* (115)

Considering the nature of the task and its predominantly intellectual emphasis, Learned proposed a new name: "*preceptor.*" He liked this better than tutor because it was less familiar. Whatever the label used to describe such a guide however, Learned insisted that the name should carry an unambiguous force and weight as an integral and, to the freshman, a dominating feature of college life. He felt that selection, training, and corporate sense of mission of the "preceptors" was the single most important business of the college with the freshman. He described the mission like this:

> To befriend a young mind, to interpret correctly its background, to explore its qualities in systematic discussion, to make clear to it those forces of intellectual activity that it will be likely to find most profitable and inviting, and finally, to engage its imagination and the enthusiasm of its possessor for the opportunities before it—this is the essence of positive education, and can be only measurably fulfilled with the best talent that any institution can supply. To miss this fact is to miss the inherent values. (116)

The qualities to be sought for in a preceptor ought to be of the type apparent in a successful dean, for Learned looked upon the preceptors as virtually assistant deans—unimpaired, however, by characteristic administrative distractions and isolation. The preceptors should be ready to meet intellectual curiosity at any point with immediate, sympathetic, and intelligent response. They should be fired with a scholar's innate love of knowledge; the preceptor's own active interests should include the relations of departments of knowledge. "Education as a whole for any student," Learned observed, "is the affair of no mere department, and men that are incapable of the larger view even at some personal sacrifice, are of little value to a student at this point." (117)

For the college itself—and quite apart from the preceptorial function—Learned saw immense value in the selection and development of a goup of "freshman guides" representing the idea of whole education and drawn from the more mature, more experienced ranks. Through them, he felt, the institution might begin to display a coherent and unitary policy of *education* as distinguished from mere administration and from research, a policy that could be soundly arrived at only through the cooperative, individual case study of many students with widely varying needs.

What would be the functions of the freshman preceptor as successor to banished advisers? First, as viewed by the student, he becomes the responsible guide and counselor. For the time being, to the student the preceptor *is* the college. Second, as concerns the college, the preceptor becomes "the discriminating inspector of the human raw material" that comes to the campus, "the instrument whereby its ideals are inculcated, and the moulder of its policies with a view to a better individual service." The achievement of both these functions at the outset revolves chiefly around the possibility of implanting in the student a vivid notion of a definite and feasible goal toward which he can shape his course.

Learned came to believe that most definitions of college aims are made for post-college consumption, i. e., for administrators, trustees, and parents. They are therefore "heavily weighted with *imponderabilia* which are important to the older mind but confuse rather than help a student. Practical college aims to be entertained by the student," said Learned, "cannot be constructed out of imponderables; they must be *concrete, tangible,* and *measurable.*" (118)

How and where does the preceptor begin his work with the freshman? Learned explained:

The preceptor first undertakes to make the student conscious of the nature of the task before him. He makes it apparent little by little that the mere getting of lessons, the reporting from books and encyclopedias, the passing of tests, and so forth, all of which were familiar in high school, are superficial, and in some cases even worthless, performances; that his real business in college is to gather valuable ideas, to criticize them, and to arrange them with other ideas in satisfactory and defensible relations; that courses and departments are arbitrary but necessary evils, and that the student, in his thinking, should break down such artificial divisions as quickly as possible and insist upon the important underlying continuity and interdependence that does in fact exist throughout their content. (119)

But what of the freshman's qualifications for the treatment of ideas of any sort? Here Learned wanted the preceptor to get down to fundamentals by seeking answers to questions that are important to education. For example:

Can the freshman read?

Can he read a book or a paragraph only?

Can he distinguish accurately between two different but similar ideas?

Can he think independently and persistently?

Does a new idea act creatively within him?

Is he easily excited by books or ideas that have no connection with courses or credits?

How does he respond to intellectual confusion or overthrow?

Does the result rest lightly on him, or does it compel reconstruction?

Is fresh thinking in any direction a pleasurable and habitual occupation to him?

Go beneath the surface of the accepted schoolboy conventions, Learned urged. Persuade the student that the beginning of education is a disposition to think vigorously for oneself. Let the preceptor and student undertake together to explore the field of ideas and to discover those which in his case are most worth attention. Let the preceptor study the boy. Of what and to what extent is he appreciative? What are his enthusiasms, his distastes? Was his alleged fondness for literature in high school merely a personal response to an appealing teacher, or has he a real hunger for literary ideas? Is dislike of French traceable merely to bad teaching, or is all language work burdensome?

It is at this point, said Learned, that the need of an accurate account of a student's previous intellectual history and present worth becomes most pressing for guidance of his continuous intellectual voyage. Possessed of a chart of the student's growth, the preceptor, at grips with the young mind, sees at a glance precisely how that mind behaved over a period of a half dozen critical years when measured by trustworthy standards in a variety of materials. Personal facts, nonscholastic performances, health, parental influence, and general background stand on the record in black and white—from year to year—as attested by competent observers. Properly interpreted and in conjunction with what the student himself discloses, the "record" supplies an indispensable guide for the preceptor.

With friendly, sympathetic relations established and with the freshman's adolescent preconception of the methods and purpose of education up for revision, the preceptor's opportunity comes clearly into focus, namely, *"to help the student formulate for himself a concrete, intellectual purpose that he can understand and that will fire his imagination."* (120)

Into a description of that high intellectual moment of communion between the freshman and his preceptor Learned poured his own heart in these words:

This is inherently a spirited task for any thoughtful youngster who deserves the consideration of the college. The world is before him, and in its broad features, at least, everything is interesting; the drudgery does not immediately appear. The tutor's share in the performance is chiefly to be a buffer of corrective knowledge and common sense, and to prevent superficial generalizations. He must possess a feeling for the outcomes of a college education in different fields and for their implications in the form of human satisfactions, together with a just perception of the range and quality of effort that should go into them. All of this he should contrive to communicate while requiring the student to explore vigorously and exactly the main features of the intellectual map spread out before him. Some consider this semi-philosophical occupation too difficult for college freshmen—a complaint which has much to do with the present excess of external regimentation and the low degree of intelligent inner responsibility for which we hold a student accountable at this point. Anyone familiar with the academic exactions from students of like age the world over knows that *the American student is treated in both high school and college much like an intellectual infant.* (121)

What Learned had in mind was not another version of an orientation course. Heaven forbid! Even a "formal" orientation course smacked of more of the same mechanism for standard mass education. There the recipe is the same for everyone; hence, Learned observed, "it speedily becomes inappropriate to the individual and ceases to satisfy him." No, the only cure for the huge overdose of "orientation," as Learned saw it, was to replace the highly organized super-effort to make it plain to all the students at the same time "what it is all about" with a new individual, private, personal approach. "For its main springs," he observed, "an education that moves minds must depend heavily on appeals *ad hominem*." He explained why:

When the personality of the student is fully recognized and dealt with, when his peculiar ambitions are consulted and when his responsibility is sole and inevitable, then things happen with a force and inner satisfaction that are unique, and education ensues. (122)

Indeed Learned believed that a five minute personal contact between an able preceptor and a student whom he has come to understand is capable of focusing attention and generating energy that months of mere class attendance could never approach. Formalities, traditions, regulations, all can be shattered with impunity, and often with great gain, when a student and teacher are on intimate footing. Of course inspiration does occur in class when conditions are favorable, but Learned was convinced that the chances for favorable conditions are infinitely multiplied when two minds deal exclusively with each other. Sarcastically, Learned observed that the tangible fruit to be expected from so few months' work on such a program may seem small indeed, especially insignificant when "compared with the information that some admissions officers claim to derive from a three-to-ten-minute freshman interview!" (123)

Learned was not proposing freshman preceptorial comradeship for the gifted to the exclusion of the average mind. He put it this way:

Whether the student is equipped with a machine gun or a pea shooter is precisely what the college has to discover; having intelligently settled that fact and corrected the student's aim, it may well turn its major attention to those displaying the most effective weapons. (124)

Learned felt that except on the theory that college work is

a chaotic mosaic of brief, disconnected mental experiences of approximately equal value, it seems reasonable to hold that no student should be allowed, much less required, to commit himself to a course of study that professes to involve his whole education without a period of first-hand, personal self-revelation made under competent, friendly observation. (125)

In his effort to light the path for the preceptorial relationship, Learned discussed in detail the technique as he envisioned it. A preceptor's usefulness depends to a large extent on the initial assumption with which the student approaches him. Once accepted for admission, the freshman goes to his preceptor for the provisional planning of his studies *and* for registration. Thus there is no doubt in the student's mind about the preceptor's right to question and direct him; he is accepted as a matter of course like the president, dean, or class teacher. Over against this authoritative background lie the perfect freedom and informality of the preceptor's service as a personal introduction to a new stage of education. His function is to understand and to make the most out of his charges. He gives no marks or credits, has no course or syllabus to cover; he deals directly with the educational values that present themselves. Each student's problems become his problems, and through him the entire experience and resources of the institution are brought to bear.

In the interest of definite progress, Learned felt that a regular weekly meeting is probably essential. To ensure systematic and precise thinking the freshman should write out what he has to say on a given subject and read it, whether it be the review of a book or a chapter of personal experience or insight. However, liberty in the form and content of the interviews should be complete. A program or syllabus—a format—would defeat the purpose. Rather, the preceptorial method is close, pertinent discussion. Again Learned spoke from his heart:

> The genius of the procedure is to follow where the discussion leads and to interest the student in the sequence of his own thinking. Ideas that once seemed to him obvious will be disproved; what he considered absurd may presently appear natural; preconceptions will be questioned at every turn until he is forced to find an independent footing that he can defend. Gradually he should come to see that to extend this island of social ground as widely as possible through contact with books and with better minds than his own is education; it is this conviction that a skillful personal guide will press home with every opportunity. A youth who has once grasped this notion will no longer be satisfied to be exploited for a term or to toil merely for credits. In his ignorance he did both, but now he has an aim—*the enlightened aim of a self-educating individual.* (126)

If the tutorial relation is personally congenial, the freedom that it enjoys may produce the finest results in the most casual fashion. The preceptor is in a position to lift the matters in hand out of the formalized routine of the classroom; he may even disrupt the "parasitic notion of the academic bargain—a degree for 120 points." The preceptor brings "a curriculum of living ideas into their deserved place among the student's preferred concerns." (127)

To achieve its purpose the preceptorial conversation needs a locale with atmosphere. Learned described the setting as he dreamed of it like this:

> He would be a thoughtless pedagogue who would undertake such personal interviews in a bare office or classroom, or at odd moments before or after other apparently more pressing engagements. The man to whom intellectual life is really important would give his conversations with students the finest setting that he could devise, if only to enforce the perspective of worth and dignity that he was trying to

communicate. An appointment *ad hoc,* without interruption, in the most comfortable and attractive parlor or study available, and before an open fire, if possible; tea or tobacco, if desired, and then a quiet half-hour of intimate conversation with minds free to concentrate. On good days, a long walk, a canoe, perhaps a round of golf; anything to *convince the student* (and possibly the tutor) that interesting ideas constitute the real world in spite of the warped and desiccating treatment that they often receive under the artificial pressure of formal requirements. The tutor must somehow fix the notion that the college is equipped and desires to deal, in dynamic fashion, with the best that a student possesses, that ideas may not only be profitable but that they are "good form," and that the customary philistine attitude of the school and college boy is in bad taste. We have done our best to foster the opposite attitude by dealing with him only in the mass and by virtually requiring that he run with the herd; there is every reason to believe that *the moment we discriminate and make education a responsible, personal affair, kindled directly by contact with educated minds, the student will respond accordingly.* (128)

As a matter of fact, Learned foresaw that opportunities for various forms of personal consideration would have a powerful refining effect, limited only by the perceptions of the preceptor himself. Here, for example, comes

a student whose interests and abilities are chiefly scientific, although he finds himself assigned to a preceptor whose field is mathematics, which he also likes. In their discussions together, there are continually cropping up scientific matters on which the preceptor may be informed but where he lacks the voice of authority. He therefore suggests that the following week he thinks he can get the professor of chemistry to come in for a chat over the matter; or he gets the student invited to the latter's home; or he writes a personal note and makes a telephone appointment for him that will receive serious and favorable attention. In other words, he does anything in his power to ensure immediate right of way for personal intellectual problems on a level that maintains their personal and preferred status. What freshman would not be helpfully inspired to see such notice taken of his thinking? This should be the college's chief business. (129)

Here Learned added an *obiter dictum:*

As things stand now, his teachers, true sons of Martha, are cumbered with all sorts of cares to get him through their courses and through college, but they do not commune with him enough to find out whether the whole proceeding has for him personally any spiritual or intellectual significance whatever. To consult them on such matters the student must take the initiative. He must first screw up his courage; since it requires courage for an intelligent mind to lay bare in a self-sought interview ideas that, however important to him, can at best be only vague and half-formulated. He must then usually cool his heels in line before the professor's door at the public office hour. Naturally, it isn't done—not, at least. by sensitive students whom advice would most help. Such calls are confined to the bare necessities of routine demand. (130)

What Learned was persistently talking about were the advantages to the freshman of *a skillful personal assistance in helping him formulate his aims for a college course.* Few concerned with education would deny the desirability of such a preceptorial relationship, but where on the campus, the credulous inquire, can faculty members be found who possess to a degree the qualities needed for such activities, and where amid all the urgent demands for money, asks the budget officer, can funds be found to introduce the plan without too great additional expense?

Learned faced these two issues. "The proposal before us," he said, "is merely to the effect that each student entering college be provided with a personal guide who will give him serious and regular attention during the early months of his course and will keep a friendly eye out for him thereafter while he is in college." (131) Learned asserted that the preceptors of the kind to whom he refers are already there on the campus—just "regular" college teachers whose gifts permit an enlargement of their sympathies, both intellectual and personal, to the point of recognizing the student's problem as paramount and of handling it with impartial wisdom. From among the roster of potential mature and sympathetic scholars, Learned suggested the elimination of certain types. First, he would scratch out those who are inflexible or those to whom teaching is a wholly self-centered enterprise, the type, as he said, "with whom verbs of teaching ignore the old rule and govern but one accusative, namely that of the 'thing.'" (132) Second, he would pass over the "ruthless and even dishonest" brilliant teacher who seeks to dominate a "lad of parts" instead of fairly appraising and guiding him for his best interests. Contingent upon such a winnowing, Learned felt that the larger and more representative the group the better. As reason for this he said:

To have a substantial core of a large faculty actually taking deliberate thought, year by year, for the mental welfare of their beginners as they cross the threshold, instead of waiting to reform or awaken those who survive until the later years, would prove a stimulating corrective to the entire establishment. Even if taken in rotation teachers at all fitted for such personal contacts could hardly fail to profit by them. A fairly inclusive group would thus make it possible to reduce the number so that no tutor should have more than, say, ten students coming to him for a weekly conference. (133)

Assuming then that a competent group of teachers is actually available for preceptorial service, how may the college provide for their effective use? While as true experimenter, each college must work out its own approach, Learned suggested going directly to the heart of the problem:

Reduce outright the lecture and recitation hours for freshmen during the first semester by one-fifth or one-fourth—say, from fifteen semester hours to twelve. Transfer the instructors so gained to advanced courses in the upper years where they would take the place of the older men chosen as preceptors. Why not experiment in this way? [Learned queried.] Why not see whether the effect of these preceptors in removing the unfit and in building up at once the power for responsible independent work projected over a long period will not more than offset the few hours lost from class attendance?

If the claims of credit should prove too meticulous the tutorial conference could be frankly equated with a three-hour course with probably less serious compromise of truth than is involved in customary equations of that nature. "Individual assignments prepared and reported to a competent preceptor at a regular personal conference might easily be made to outweigh the usual three-hour course in class." (134) Learned saw two advantages in this plan. *First*, it would permit of no question as to the official status of the preceptorial relation since it would provide a definite place for it and assign it a function. *Second*, the cost would prove to be relatively small.

Learned sharpened up his pencil to do some serious academic budgeting. With a personal conference substituted for one freshman course, the demands of ten freshmen upon each preceptor during the first semester might run to ten hours a week which, for a professor on a nine-hour schedule, would represent not more, surely, than his customary expenditure of time for one three-hour course—lectures and preparation—during the same period. Deducting from existing service, therefore, three instruction hours for each ten students, a class of one hundred freshmen would create a deficit of thirty semester hours of instruction to replace the preceptorial service given by the older men. Part of this deficit would be made up by reducing the freshman schedule, as already discussed, from fifteen semester hours to twelve.

> Thus in the case of one hundred freshmen in five sections of, say, twenty students each, this change would release these teachers from fifteen semester hours; larger sections would naturally produce a smaller saving. The other fifteen hours could be supplied, temporarily at least, by a two thousand dollar instructor teaching normally twelve hours a week. This would require about three-fifths of his annual teaching time and would cost, therefore, about $1,200, an outlay of $12.00 per student. (135)

Allowing the full freshman program of fifteen hours with the tutorial function superadded, at the rate mentioned, the cost would be about double the amount stated, and would gradually increase with the salaries paid to the new instructors. That represents roughly an investment of $2,500 for each one hundred freshmen. Such an expenditure would at least inaugurate the undertaking even with existing student programs undisturbed!

In making such calculations as these, however, as Learned pointed out, he had left wholly out of account the spontaneous interest and natural goodwill of the average faculty when confronted with a promising suggestion. Many college teachers, he believed, are already giving more time to individual student relations, formal and informal, than he proposed. "A college," he said,

> would be a sorry place were it not for the leavening influences of these casual and voluntary contacts on the part of men and women who often consider them the best portion of their service. Teachers who are most inclined to such activity are likely to be those who understand and do it best. For them a definite preceptorial relation would simply make it necessary to systematize and concentrate the time already spent in this manner. Others would be attracted to the arrangement whereby personal contacts with students would be redeemed from a largely social and irrelevant content and placed upon a natural footing by intellectual interchange. Still others who might have much to give but for whom adjustment to the individual student seems difficult, might be willing to cooperate for at least a season in the trial of a promising plan. (136)

There would be gain, Learned felt, if some professors even sacrificed personal research, outside lecturing, and other nonteaching activities, and could therefore in the nature of the case be only temporary. The project itself would, however, constitute "a piece of cooperative internal research, the consequences of which might well transform the institution as an educational agency." (137)

The first experience of a group of preceptors seeking to deal with the varied problems of whole students, instead of with departmental segments of individuals, would, Learned was convinced, bring the men together for frequent conference. This result would provide a large advantage. The meetings would tend to produce "a corporate consciousness for education as a whole that fails the modern higher institution almost completely." The preceptors, being selected and experienced men any of whom might presumably be "competent deans," should have power as individuals to bring about, in behalf of their assigned students, such changes as they might feel to be in their interests. Unusual measures might be referred to a committee or to the dean for final decision, but in general the tutor should understand that the program upon which he and a given student might agree would, if possible, be carried out." (138) The preceptor's powers ought eventually to include, Learned thought, the omission or deferment of prescribed courses, the selection of unusual electives, the addition of an extra course, the granting of listener's privileges, or, as the desired end, the outlining of an entirely individual four-year curriculum built to fit the student's special needs. Thus the tutor would bear the responsibility for a determinative analysis of the freshman's problems. Learned was frank to say that schedules growing out of this process should at least compare favorably with the present regime in which

> formally standardized requirements conceal innumerable fallacious assumptions of knowledge, while in many cases they deny essential justice. A physician asked to prescribe *en masse* for the entire population of a hospital would face a problem not essentially more difficult than that which the college professors attempt to solve annually with the customary generalized prescription, or election, of its courses. (139)

Of one requirement Learned was certain: the preceptorial procedure would require wise and skillful guidance in proportion as it succeeded in departing from the mere mechanical routine against which it is directed. Hence there would need to be a responsible head of the group—call him what you will—whose duty it would be to unite his colleagues in a common conception of their function, to devise and exchange methods of dealing with students, and to build a valid foundation, case by case, for the sort of education that the institution purposes to give. In selecting or relieving tutors, or in transferring students from one tutor to another, his authority should be extensive. Personal relations between student and preceptor should at all costs be kept on a footing of sound and friendly confidence, an intimacy which the student ought to know will never be used except to his advantage. "For developing this general morale among both preceptors and students, the supervision of a chief preceptor would be indispensable." (140)

Learned proposed the preceptorial program as a substitute for "a cunningly devised mechanism of education set up more or less with the hope that it will run itself, a group of persons who are educators in fact and who will confront and deal with what are wholly individual problems in a responsible personal manner." (141) Without some such intelligent linkage between a student's past and an uncharted future, the problem of transition from high school to college seemed to Learned, for many students, to be insoluble.

Learned summarized his preceptorial concept by saying that

> a real college is a place where, for both students and teachers, life from the very outset is heavily interwoven with opportunities, chiefly informal, for exchanging ideas, for giving and absorbing inspiration, and for letting the wealth and vigor of fine spirits prevail over that which is perfunctory and commonplace. *The purpose of the freshman tutor is, without wasting a moment, to initiate the new student into college life as thus conceived, and to give him the courage and the habitual impulse to make the most of it.* (142)

6

THE ALIEN REQUIREMENT

Ritual of the Mark

Upon analysis of the statistical results of the Pennsylvania study Learned came to believe that what he labeled the "package method" of academic advancement had served its purpose in American higher education. He looked hopefully upon the passing of the system of units and credits which, useful as it had been in the early 1900s, "is not good enough for American education today." (143)

Without exploring the moral implications of academic fraud created by competition for marks or the wholesale cheating engendered by the system, Learned rested his case for reform on the extensive evidence which the studies produced to show the appalling discrepancy between a student's demonstrable knowledge and his ability as recognized by grades given him by his instructors. Under the ritual of the mark, said Learned, "the sole question is whether by hook or crook one can pass the arbitrary dead line with a collection of tokens that are likewise arbitrary." (144)

The substitution of a numerical symbol for an assumed intellectual value became increasingly repugnant to him. He expressed his position in these words:

> Any attempt to measure individual achievement on the basis of time spent or teachers' term grades, as now given to students in large groups and insufficiently understood, is in great measure a futile and ironic practice; these hour and unit standards based on subjective estimates of unassimilated information, contain no assurance of important meaning, and should not be used to measure an educational product when anything better is available. (145)

Learned's indictment stemmed from the fact that a mechanical goal measured by an adding machine computation in the registrar's office

> depends on a mechanical apparatus for its achievement. Once set up, without clear educational objectives stated in educational terms, a fixed machine for producing supervised term credits, however they may be reckoned, tends to *exclude everything not organized within the courses offered.* (146)

To describe such an educational system Learned coined the phrase *"self-sufficient indifference of the teaching mechanism."* (147)

Learned's concern about the meaning of academic grades was a part of his whole questioning of segmentation and discontinuity of the individual's knowledge. Looked at from the point of view of the student as the alleged beneficiary, the educational process appeared to Learned as if we were attempting to erect a sixteen-story building with

> wholly different architects, contractors, and designs for the first six, the second six, and the last four floors. The workmen at the thirteenth story scarcely inquire whether the substructure has been of steel, bricks, or wooden posts, provided it has reached the regulation height; and as for continuity, any one of their standard patterns—a hall, a museum, a library—is cheerfully undertaken regardless of whether the lines rising from below imply a residence, an office building, or a cathedral. (148)

It was Learned's belief that education can rarely be genuine and also tidy in the administrator's sense. The practice of assuming the formal identity of achievement expressed in credits might provide "administrative peace of mind," but created "far-reaching" damage in a "professed equating of educational content by means of the standardized wrappings in which it is delivered." (149) He believed that a movement toward educational sanity would require a shift in the very center of institutional gravity. He made his indictment specific:

> To anyone who knows the facts, it is evident that, in spite of the

friendly attitude of teachers and the helpless good wishes of deans, *our educational institutions are interested in pupils and students only where they happen to impinge upon the formal operations of the mechanism.* We cannot tolerate administrative vagueness, suspense, or untidiness in our education. We must "know where we are" in good clean credits even though the pupils get nowhere in particular. In other words, *we are afraid frankly to place the student, always unique and highly variable, in the full focus of attention and to venture direct dealings with the elusive, but recognizable and supremely desirable thing that we know true education to be.* We set enormous store by curricula and instruction, as though these were the essential matters, instead of bending every effort, first of all, toward finding out what unique combination of forces each individual before us actually presents, what he is, what he knows, what he wants to do, what he can do, what he probably should do; then helping him to do his own learning under conditions that keep him in constant contact with the realities of his progress. (150)

In the organic discontinuity of the process of American higher education Learned found "the mark" playing an officially deceptive role. It satisfies the administrative desire to have student affairs in order. It discharges the teacher from further responsibility for the student. It provides the student with a calendar for time-serving purposes and provides a schedule to indicate whether he is moving according to the timetable to get out of college with a diploma and a degree. It moves the student socially up the class rank from freshman to senior. *A student as a registrar's statistic becomes a convenient homogeneous administrative analogue.*

Although Learned recognized that a thorough reconstruction of the college would have to take its point of departure from premises fundamentally different from the prevailing ones, he was aware of the wholesale implications of his suggestions. What, for example, becomes of the college class defined as those who happen to enter at the same date "if each person is to be faithfully explored and developed for the unique quantity, value, and force of his ideas?" (151) Is perhaps such encouraged emphasis as "class solidarity" not mischievous? Has perhaps the value of class spirit not been imparted to the campus to fill a vacuum created by the absence of a community of intellectual interests? Or again, "what, in turn, becomes of the smaller class—or section—unit that now marches in chain-gang formation from the beginning to the end of a term, dragging with it many who derive little or no profit from its operations, because they are either too far behind or too far ahead." Obviously, said Learned,

> such a conception of instruction dies with the outworn device that has ruined, and will always ruin, group instruction, namely the *term credit*. With no credits to be earned or lost at the end, there is no virtue in keeping an advanced student within a particular group, or in urging that one who is unprepared shall stick in hopes that a lenient teacher will eke out the needed points. (152)

Learned pointed out that far from critically appraising the student, marks are given for a multitude of partly intellectual jobs, each with its frame of special conditions fixed by the teacher. In the process of checking the execution of these items, from course to course, the student, as a growing entity known to any intelligent observer, disappears. What happens is clear. Take two familiar types of youth. Case one is a student who starts brilliantly and lapses into indifference. Case two is a student who for lack of money or adequate preparation begins far down but gains steadily and comes to the top in scholarship and character. Average the marks of each for the quadrennium, and the midpoint is identical. Although obviously both marks are theoretical abstracts, they are in a form which the college accepts and promptly turns over to honor societies for their guidance. Nevertheless each tells a glaring untruth about its subject on the critical issue of his education.

Learned was convinced that one gets near the realities of personal education when one centers attention directly on the student, using the curriculum merely as a whetstone on which to perfect his edge. Accept each student as unique, Learned pleaded. Proceed to explore him. At the outset and from time to time turn his mind inside out to see what is really there. Use the data so developed to guide teaching efforts as well as to heighten the student's sense of security in what he knows and his respect both for its possession and for its increase. Lift student appraisal and decisions dealing with the core of education from easy formulas, bred of the adding machine, to the more difficult level of conclusions befitting the subject. Remember that, in spite of illusions to the contrary, the only outcome of schooling that persists beyond graduation lies not in what high or low "marks" make the student appear to have done to the curriculum; "it lies in what his studies, his teachers, the whole sum of his activities, in reality did to him. When the alumnus searches his heart, it is on this point that the college is finally judged." (153)

To Learned, reaching back into his German experience and deep into the Carnegie statistical records, the chief evil in the American college examination seemed to be the immediacy with reference to what it tests. It provides an incentive to remember a lot of facts as they looked in the textbook—until the semester or course examination gives official permission to forget them. With characteristic vividness Learned put his point like this:

A fresh supply of raw facts heaped up by a cramming process for official inspection and credit on the books, tells us little or nothing. What we need to know is how much of that mass will be digested. We naively assume that the impressive contents of some thirty-two high school courses and forty odd college courses measure the education of the student who traverses them; at no point do we seek to find out what these injections have actually become in terms of durable educational tissue. It is this ultimate product that should have chief attention. (154)

Learned thought it essential that the idea of testing should be kept so far from any particular educational exercise that the pupil is not misled by it. Why? because

his business is to understand the matter in hand; to follow its implications to the limit of his interest. His appreciation and response should be engrossed with the intrinsic merits of the ideas before him. Therein lies his permanent education as distinguished from superficial reactions intended to justify "credits." If this cannot be done; if he can only be moved by fearing some nameless fate that lurks in "flunking," then he is probably working with the wrong stuff. The last thing that should occur to him is that the matter presented must be remembered until examination. This is no purist's criticism of his motive; it is simply to recognize the fact that knowledge held in place by such considerations does not last. It is, in general, not worth measuring. (155)

He wanted no examination-dominated curriculum in the sense of registering semester by semester what has been laid out in advance. He said:

We need to exorcize the haunting fear of an impending test that is geared to a multitude of items which as yet have little perspective or significance to the student and over which he worries lest one escape. . . . Sealing a course with a test and a credit is like putting a candle that has just been lighted in a dark room; one hastily notes down what one has only vaguely seen and hardly understood. A "course" should involve no immediate, conclusive tests; it should simply open wide a door to light up a strange apartment. . . . Above all, no test should be used, as now, to put a fateful period to a pupil's first confused impressions. Tests on new stuff may, of course, be given, but only as an aid, a standing invitation to return later when knowledge has matured, and when the test may reveal the pupil's athomeness within areas often revisited. (156)

What kind of tests and examinations then did Learned have in mind? He described his concept explicitly! He wanted a test

which by its very structure informs the student and keeps him aware of the whole subject with which it deals—its elements, its central relationships, its more typical implications, its fastest growing developments. Books and courses turn on lights. The important thing is the actual thinking the student does for himself about what he sees. This the tests should measure and should have no necessary relation to any courses. It is appropriate, therefore, to hold tests periodically available to the student over the whole range of knowledge regardless of his school program. The purpose of the teacher and the college is to arouse and intensify the student's thinking in as many fields as his personal energy and ability find profitable. (157)

To Learned it was essential that the comprehensive inventories which he championed should not have an immediate connection with any particular item on any particular day in such a way as to defeat a student's intent to understand a matter for its own sake. His record examinations were to require and reward a true intellectual poise rather than a feverish obsession with "marks." It would be a test not only of matured knowledge but also of the motivation that produces it. Learned believed that when the tests of a student's success no longer rest with teacher's marks but measure with approximate accuracy the amount of profitable thinking done, ideas mastered, working knowledge retained, the chief duty of the college will become unmistakable. And what would be that indicated task?

To exhaust every resource in finding for each student that magic area in which "profitable thinking" can and will be done, ideas be mastered, and working knowledge retained. For some, the materials must be simplified, for others greatly advanced, but when the test is applied and gains or losses revealed, one fact must infallibly appear: *the school must ensure that what is measured is the pupil's permanent capital, with power behind it and a use to make of it.* (158)

With his optimistic faith in the positive response of students to education redeemed from the ritual of the mark, now solidly strengthened by his research data developed in the Pennsylvania study, Learned asserted the proposition that the student will be the first to seek and endorse the intellectual inventory, successor to the alien requirement of the mark. The inventory profile, he asserted, becomes

as inevitable and significant as the mark that registers his high jump or the time that measures his 100 yards. (159)

Learned looked to the refinement of the tools for measurement as an avenue for education to escape from the pseudo-standards that hamper and mislead higher education. Increasing knowledge of measurement, he was convinced, would one day encourage the college to be sound and bold enough to shift its emphasis from formal instruction on which a student is minutely judged and credited, to a searching analysis of the student and to his aid in acquiring an education founded on demonstrable resources. Then, he felt, the simple, necessary, and drastic revolution would ensue;

education would restore *the sense of achievement in its own terms—namely, the mastery of important knowledge.* He said:

> Let us have done with credits, points, semester hours, units, and the like, and let us act on our conviction that education consists in awareness of the insights that result from essential interlocking ideas thoroughly understood. *We shall thereby have touched off the charge that must clear the way for all the rest.* (160)

From his intimate Pennsylvania experience in the largest educational measurement study undertaken up to his time—"a project embarked upon with the greatest misgivings and only because it appeared to afford the best chance of a helpful solution" to education's gravest problems—Learned stated as his informed conclusion that more can be done "for the sanitation" of the educational processes through objective educational measurement, intelligently developed and applied, than in any other way. (161) Speaking with authority as a responsible Carnegie staff officer as well as a pioneer in a new educational territory, he declared that "we already know that *the travesty of college scholarship that is permitted today is wholly needless. If it is retained it is simply because we intend to retain a travesty.*" (162)

As his considered conclusion Learned asserted that the ritual of the mark injects an alien requirement into the educational process that is destructive of intellectual morale. He put his idea like this:

> The basis of *intellectual morale* is to be found solely in the grip that sequences of important, educative ideas have on the mind. *The prerequisites for its development are time, freedom, and encouragement to continuous thought*—all elements that are conspicuously lacking in colleges as at present organized. (163)

7

THE GRADUATE RECORD EXAMINATION

Profile of Permanent and Available Equipment

The *Graduate Record Examination,* which today has a place as accepted on the academic calendar as Christmas and Easter holidays, was conceived in the mind of William S. Learned as a pilot project. Designed originally as a practical means for determining the fitness of applicants for advanced study at Harvard, Princeton, Yale, and Columbia, it was to provide both an immediately usable tool and the "kind of" trustworthy measuring rod which Learned felt necessary to liberate American teaching and learning from slavery to the tidy bookkeepers who so easily become lords of the campus manor.

The development of the Graduate Record Examination consumed Learned's major energies during the most mature years of his educational thinking and research. Its practical usefulness to graduate admission officers became so immediate and his duties related to its extension and administration so complex that his retirement arrived before he had stimulated the kind of responsible and responsive college program which could best be served by it. The record examinations, spelled in the plural and in lower case, stood, however, ready for further usefulness.

In retrospect some educators remember Learned as a cold, meticulous test technician. Nothing could be further from the truth. Learned was essentially a philosopher; to him the Graduate Record Examination was merely one tool designed to implement the concept of education in which he believed. The test was no more the final object of his concern than the use of the T square is the purpose of an architect drawing plans for a house or the manipulation of a plumb line the purpose of the builder. Learned's intellectual inventory, of which the record examination was a demonstration model, provided merely an educational instrument with a sharper edge. Ben Wood says that he and Learned felt that "until something better is discovered, objective tests represent an *essential* but not a sufficient source of information about the abilities, interests, and needs of individual pupils."

The record examination *idea* with which Learned's name is so historically identified was rooted in his fundamental belief that the intellectual career of the student should be determined not only by his capacity but by his progressive attainment in the field of enduring knowledge. This, he reiterated in and out of season, involves less emphasis upon administrative techniques of the unit-credit type and more emphasis upon the individual student.

Learned provided the early and strongest stimulus toward the growth of objective testing programs in higher education. Thus he stood as a central figure in the movement which led to the remarkable improvement in the utility and trustworthiness of examinations. The experience with the new type of objective testing, which emerged from the Pennsylvania study, did much to meet the heavy demands for educational appraisal which followed the return of the GI students to the campus.

Ten years after the Pennsylvania study was undertaken the Graduate Record Examination program was initiated in 1937 under the sponsorship of the four major graduate schools in collaboration with the Carnegie Foundation for the Advancement of Teaching with funds supplied by the Carnegie Corporation of New York. The project was inaugurated as an experiment. In the beginning it was owned and completely controlled by the four deans of the founding graduate schools.

During the period of Learned's work with the tests the foundation at a cost of over three million dollars financed some three dozen studies involving the use of tests and measurements. The

Pennsylvania study was the first to be attempted at the college level on a wide-scale basis. It demonstrated the feasibility of using objective-type tests for evaluation of student learning in college. Even more significant was its establishment of the principle of measuring such learning in different colleges with a common yardstick or battery of achievement tests. In objective testing at the college level, Learned's wisdom, insights, and influence have stood the rigorous test of time. In the years since the tests were developed, a number of technical and other improvements have been made in the GRE. The tests, which since 1948 have been conducted by the Educational Testing Service, however, are still designed to measure the knowledge acquired by students in the common program of liberal arts by a series of tests in major fields of study, continue to evaluate the college student's progress toward the two major objectives stipulated by Learned, namely (1) intellectual growth and development through the study of the liberal arts and (2) the achievement of mastery in a selected field of specialization.

Learned, it needs to be pointed out, was solely responsible for the conception, planning, and organization of the Pennsylvania study. When he first talked with Ben Wood about the immediate purpose of showing by a massive sampling that there was a real need for more accurate and more comparable measure of the abilities and achievements of students, the general plan and purposes of the project were already clear in Learned's mind. Learned invited Ben Wood to become his assistant charged with the technical implementation of the project, chiefly in the matter of selecting and producing the objective tests used in the study, of supervising the administration and scoring of the tests, and of planning and carrying out the basic statistical analysis of the test scores. On the basis of statistical evidence supplied by Wood, Learned wrote every line, except for table and chart legends, in the series of reports which flowed from the research. (164)

While the concern with the testing program produced a better educational measuring instrument, this essential by-product was a step toward Learned's major concern: how objective test results could be recorded in combination with other relevant information about individual pupils so as to be interpreted and *used* conveniently for the benefit of students considered as *individuals*.

When Learned and Wood undertook the project to show by the massive sampling the need for more accurate and comparable measures of evaluation, testing, both because of its strangeness and imperfections, and because of the extravagant claims made for tests by their authors, enjoyed a growing ill-repute. Learned's activity helped to turn the tide and enabled objective tests to take their place as accepted tools in the educational process.

Utilizing the objective question technique, which as late as 1940 was still being referred to as the "new type," Learned proposed to develop an examination which would insure comparability and a wide sampling within a reasonable time period of six hours or two half days. He proposed to give uniform tests in various fields and to describe the examinee by a configuration of his achievement over the entire series which should constitute his "curve" or "profile."

In the beginning the subjects were divided into A and B level groups. Eight relatively elementary tests constituted the A level, namely: mathematics, physics, chemistry, biology, history and government, literature, fine arts, and a verbal factor. The B level pattern was comprised of tests in thirteen fields of undergraduate specialization, namely: philosophy, psychology, economics, government, history, mathematics, physics, chemistry, geology, biology, English literature, French, and the fine arts. The elementary examination, not being pitched at a specific standard, was so graded as appropriately to distribute the entire number of examinees—except the students who have specialized in that field. These naturally gravitated to the top. The advanced examination was so graded as to distribute similarly those who had majored in a given subject, or those whom the elementary test failed to stop.

While the construction of these examinations became the main focus, a pattern of collaboration was established to insure that the content of each test would be reasonably satisfactory to each institution. Thus the task of making the test in a given field was lodged with a committee consisting of four professors in that subject, one appointed from each institution by the respective deans. In the first fifteen months of the construction of the advanced tests, some 60 regular committee members collaborated. If colleagues brought in as critics, consultants, outside experts of similar rank who contributed material are included, some 145 individuals drawn from 20 institutions were involved in test development.

Because of interest in the historical development of the test as well as its working usefulness, a review of a typical working agenda of a test committee has value.

1. Preliminary discussions
   A. Purpose, conditions, and limitations of the test.
   B. Desirable balance and proportions of content to be used.
   C. Most useful types of questions considered.
2. Consideration of provisional questions—several times the number required being prepared.
   A. By committee members.
   B. By experts employed by the committee.
3. Editing of provisional questions.
   A. Draft sent to committee members for individual criticism and revision.
   B. Committee members return draft with answers.
4. Collation and reissuance of answers and criticisms.
   A. Elimination of questions with variant answers.
   B. Revision of questions with variant answers.
5. Selection of preliminary test.
   A. Items tried out on students as representative as possible of the students eventually to be tested.
6. Analysis of pretest results.
   A. For the whole test.
   B. For the behavior of each item.

Operating along the lines of such an agenda, Learned's committees prepared and defended *the first examination of its type ever to be constructed at its level.* The norms used in the experimental period were not mere blanket averages of all those who participated. Rather, they were averages made up from as homogeneous groups as could be assembled out of the total with a view to securing a rational base for determining individual variation. The Graduate Record Examination from the beginning was concerned with measuring a student in each of a variety of traits against a norm that had as definite a meaning as possible. It was not intended to measure one student against another with a single heterogeneous sum of his scores that might or might not fully represent him. Moreover, it was *not* intended to rank institutions among themselves by means of mass scores whose significance was not clear.

The focus of the whole endeavor, as far as Learned was concerned, remained the *individual student.* It proposed to show him and those who worked in his behalf how his organized intellectual resources compare with those of his mates in a standard college group and with those of his colleagues in a special field. The purpose of the test was to *describe the student;* to map *his* ignorance as fully as *his knowledge;* to take account not solely of courses *he* might have pursued, but to learn to what extent courses, private reading, family background, travel, and above all *his* habitual thinking, might have contributed to equip *him* with durable and useful mental furniture.

Learned was especially concerned with a quality within the test which he called "durability." He wanted a type of examination which would not reward the sort of cramming that has become familiar in "short college courses" and the *ad hoc* quizzes that polish them off. He insisted on fields so broad and a sampling so extensive that achievement would much more likely reflect a matured understanding of the subject than a response to fleeting ideas caught in a merely visual memory. Learned was convinced that students sensed and respected the element of genuineness in a test which detaches itself from the usual sources of markings and ratings; which goes below the surface and probes a mind for resources that are effectively working. He felt that the record examination, for the first time, afforded students a comparative inventory, which however merciless it might seem at certain points, was felt by the student to approximate an estimate he felt just.

While the accumulating statistical data developed by the administration of the Graduate Record Examination provided new insight into test construction, Learned on his own was winnowing the evidence to find out its bearing on basic hypotheses he held. The foremost of these was that *thinking should be cumulative.* Presumably college is dealing with ideas that if retained would constitute a permanent asset in a student's mental equipment. It worried Learned to see how generally colleges encourage a student to throw overboard power and skill acquired *en route,* together with the tools themselves, instead of adding them in orderly fashion in the student's arsenal of resources for a future in which they are potential factors. Learned felt that the college tends to have a "negative effect" because it offers no systematic appraisal and recognition for continuing achievement aside from certain sequences in its formal requirements. He explained his expectation like this:

> A lad loves mathematics and does well in it but in college turns to literature, art or history. He soon cannot help but feel that he has closed the door forever on a set of dynamic ideas that he would gladly use but that are rapidly drifting out of reach. Here is a student of economics who knows little science and has no time for courses in it; but during the summer he reads and rereads a book on geology. Suppose these two men knew that four or five times in the progress of their college experience they would meet an opportunity to display precisely the extent to which those mathematical concepts had been retained or enlarged; or, in comparison with others who took courses, just how far the careful reading of a text-book advances one in geology. What difference would gradually creep into their attitude toward the cultivation of the whole web of interrelated human ideas? I should predict that *within a college generation a live faculty willing to buttress the idea of maintaining an open, active, and retentive mind* instead of issuing a standing invitation to parcel out, to write off, and to forget, *could effect a visible change in intellectual morale due to this innovation alone.* (165)

Well before Pearl Harbor, Learned had given a good deal of thought to the place which the record type of examination ought to play in an effective scheme of institutional education. He hopefully assumed that the tendency of higher education was away from the minute educational bookkeeping of the past with its storage of symbols for courses traversed and teachers appeased, to a concern with the present outfit with which a mind, eager to display its present powers and worth, might be equipped. What Learned envisioned was a continuing, expanding process in which stimulating supervision and inspection of the values actually developed and permanently acquired would replace the motivation heretofore expected from accumulating course credits. By the use of the record examinations, Learned felt that a consistent and trustworthy measure of a student's *quantitative* gains for his reading and thinking in every field he touches would be measured. The test, he felt, would help to keep apart objective and subjective appraisal. He put his thought like this:

> Knowledge, information, judgment, problem-solving ability—all these stages are handled progressively throughout a student's college career, as routine procedure having nothing to do specifically with what he studies. As he thinks and reads and listens these great main reservoirs steadily fill up. Measurement therein must be taken repeatedly and so adjusted as to secure his maximum performance. This sort of thing a student understands and welcomes. It is a gauge of his accumulating interest-bearing capital. It stimulates him to keep his mind open and curious but it doesn't interfere in the least with any educational exercise.
>
> On the other hand, the quality of a student's performance emerges solely in response to interaction with his teachers and his fellows. It is entirely shortsighted to tie this down to what he can put on paper on a Monday morning in May of his senior year. It should be a continuing verdict assembled by those who know him, and he should be judged by the very best things he can produce when the thoughts are ripe and the mood is on. Here, it seems to me, is the point at which we can release the student and the professor from ulterior considerations and let them revel in the high values of their joint undertaking, the student fully aware that there is nothing to concern him except the depth and scope of his own insight. . . .
>
> If in this age of informality and directness we can forget the mechanical formulas that have oppressed us, it is not unlikely that we shall find the channels of a student's most effective education to coincide with the most trustworthy sources of judgment as to a student's worth. (166)

It needs to be emphasized that Learned took his point of departure from that view that education is unavoidably intellectual. Education, he asserted, consists in thinking, in the perception of meanings and relationships among ideas which are true and important, and in the marshaling of an individual's natural emotions behind ideas in proportion to their truth and importance. Moreover he was of the opinion that each new level of intellectual performance must of necessity be based on root foundations below. Thus, each current program would incorporate the knowledge, skill, and power acquired previously, in a more complex intellectual performance which would assume and utilize the equipment which a student brought into the effort. In such a spirally ascending knowledge-skill-power model, the student would grow in intellectual poise—and that growth would surely be reflected on the record examinations.

Learned felt that semester courses of study rounded up with a credit examination have bred in the American student the academic illusion that he is dealing with knowledge. No, said Learned, a mass of crammed and undigested information visually recalled, deposited, and abandoned *is one of the chief preventives of education.* Information is not knowledge until it is fitted permanently into the structure of an individual's mind. To deserve recognition, knowledge must be a relatively permanent and available equipment of the student. It must be so familiar and so sharply defined that it comes freely to mind when needed and can be depended on as an effective cross-fertilizing element for producing fresh ideas. He never suggested that a student does not need to know facts. He wanted, however, to see the facts developed into trunk-line ideas that carry a subject and can only be mastered by being given time to grow. So much did he emphasize this point that he asserted that genuine review is the "essence of learning." (167) He stated his feeling like this:

> Genuine review . . . is the sculptor facing his clay; he reviews it every time he looks at it to change, add, or subtract. Exactly the same is the attitude of any learner toward the central structure of ideas which he refines and extends as fresh thoughts come to him from instruction, whether from books or persons, or from observation.

The clarity and perspective of these central ideas have everything to do with their permanence. Bad education denies this; it crowds a lot of dismembered notions into a succession of small spaces; it examines and marks the pupil on each, then dismisses them and passes him along for more. Good education selects large, simple ideas which transcend the limit of terms or year; good education builds these ideas gradually into his permanent possession and shows how they fit and control other ideas; it teaches where to hang the details on these main conceptions, and by constant review, as the sculptor reviews his clay, it gives the pupil a sure feeling for what is important and what is irrelevent—*a genuine philosophy*. Steadily built up in this fashion, sound idea-structures result from the pupil's own creation, independent of teacher and school; demanding expression and growth, they constitute an equipment that makes the present accumulation of "marks" a sorry substitute. (168)

To Learned the record examination was never an end, but always a means to project a trustworthy incentive toward cumulative, personalized, intellectual growth. For the student the examination provided a lever to extricate and liberate him from the mind-suffocating private accounting system carried on by the registrar's adding machine. The profile provided a chart which could be used in guiding further growth. By means of the record examinations considered as an instrument within the context of a thoroughly re-structured pattern of higher education, Learned felt that the intellectual growth of the individual student would emerge as the primary goal in a continuing intellectual voyage of on-going self-education. The real business of the student wherever he is found, as Learned saw it, is "systematic and profitable thinking." (169)

While the incentive to the development of the Graduate Record Examination lay in the desire of four great graduate schools to find a trustworthy and objective means for determining the capabilities of a rising tide of applicants, an unforeseen need for its utilization presented itself before the experimental period was scarcely completed. By 1944 the problem of the returning soldier directed toward graduate or professional study was becoming acute as a substantial government entitlement enabled the veteran to apply at the institution of his choice and leave the task of admission and adjustment to the institution. To Learned the essential question to be asked of the veteran was this: "Does he possess an equipment in ideas, understood and digested, that can be quickly refreshed and increased to the point of proficiency in the career he proposes to follow?" (170)

By the time of Learned's retirement in 1946 some 150 colleges, graduate schools, and professional divisions were requiring or recommending the use of the Graduate Record Examination. It had become the negotiable gold coin of academic value. In addition to his work on the project, Learned had given indispensable help and encouragement in the founding and development of the Educational Records Bureau; the National Teacher Examination Project; the college Sophomore Testing Program; and the development of aptitude tests for various professions. With Ben Wood he was influential in persuading Thomas J. Watson, of the International Business Machines Corporation, to develop the first automatic test scoring machine which literally revolutionized the whole testing movement, providing timely aid to meet educational wartime requirements.

All the time, however, Learned was quietly at work in drafting the original plan for the merger of the nonprofit testing agencies. *The Educational Testing Service, located in Princeton, as a major instrumentality of American education, continues to demonstrate the permanence of the test pioneering and organizational imagination of William S. Learned.* His work thus had the quality of durable usefulness.

8

LEARNED AMONG HIS CONTEMPORARIES

The Place of the Mind in the World of Machines and Experts

In opening his Inglis Lecture at Harvard (1931) on *The Way Out of Educational Confusion* the year before Learned delivered his paper on *Realism in American Education* (1932), John Dewey observed that American society found itself "in the midst of great educational uncertainty, one probably unparalleled at any past time." (171)

Amid that uncertainty in the educational circles with which he so intimately worked, Learned pursued his staff studies with an apparent unconcern about the theories and practices set in motion by his contemporaries. He confined his operations to a limited universe defined by the objectives of his current assignment. Except by an occasional general comment in defense of a position important to his research, he rarely took note of controversy. Even then his comments were never *ad hominem*. From the heat of the discussion of his decades he kept his distance. He had his own work to do—and he concentrated on it. He submitted his reports to the profession as a brief of his position. There he left the matter.

If the date of the installation of Alexander Meiklejohn as president of Amherst College may be taken for purposes of calendar orientation as the beginning of the era in educational experimentation, it is apparent that Learned's active career spanned some thirty years of profound scrutiny of the process of higher education. At the beginning of the 1930's Abraham Flexner summarized his view of the educational situation by saying that

> no sound or consistent philosophy, thesis, or principle lies beneath the American university of today. (172)

Harry D. Gideonse gave it as his opinion that

> in the defense of a free society in America, education has become a battleground for those who think of the school as an instrument of public policy and for those who regard it as an institution for the development of the potentialities of our youth and for the unfettered pursuit of knowledge. (173)

In his inaugural address Meiklejohn had asserted that the mission of the teacher is to lead his student into the "life intellectual." "The college," he said, "is primarily not a place of the body, nor of the feelings, nor even of the will; it is, first of all, a place of the mind. . . . To be liberal a college must be essentially intellectual." (174) Learned entertained the same conviction, namely that "all education is unavoidably intellectual." (175)

From the time that he caught the scent of the intellectual purpose of education in Prussia in 1909–1910, Learned tracked it through the decades like a bloodhound determined to quarry the object of his search. He belonged to no school of thought; indeed by most contemporary schools of thought he was looked upon as a sort of free-lancing educational nonconformist incapable of sectarian classification. In an age of strong currents of idealism, realism, and pragmatism in the arena of philosophic discussion of the aims and outcomes of American education, he asserted the primacy of a "knowledge that is power" of a kind that "presupposes a mind actively at work and bent on the process of self-education." (176) His method was empirical, increasingly statistical, and always very much his own. From the beginning, it was based on comparative criticism and institutional inquiry. As educational hypotheses began to shape up from his cumulative surveys, he reached for new tools, technical associates to carry forward experiment within *his* frame of reference, and situations which would provide a universe for *his* inquiry. In this sense

Learned's entire performance possesses a singular continuity from the publication of *The Oberlehrer* to the establishment of the *Educational Testing Service*.

William Learned had no close associates or disciples. His staff work had no roots in any permanent academic setting. He entertained no desire to see an experimental college founded to incorporate his suggestions. A procession of presidents of Carnegie Corporation of New York and of the Carnegie Foundation for the Advancement of Teaching wrote prefaces to his reports and took no further action. At his death the foundation did not even have a photograph, a definitive biography, a complete set of his writings, or a summary of his findings available for convenient educational use. In his research cell at 522 Fifth Avenue he remained aloof from the personalities and controversies of his times. With a diffidence born of a natural shyness and accentuated by a courtesy with respect to the ideas of others, he published his reports and waited, often with pathetic expectancy, for a kindly gesture of response from the educational public. A procession of educators came to his office, took copies of his reports, and passed on. At the Century Club he sat in on distinguished luncheon conversations and mostly listened. His private papers show that he was in touch with the principal educational thinkers and movements of his time. His professional loneliness, however, was confided only to his wife in the quiet of their Riverside Drive apartment. It is also apparent in inferences from his correspondence. A few examples will suffice to indicate how Learned's expectations about the impact of his reports were shattered. In 1927 Carnegie "Bulletin Number Twenty" published as a whole papers first printed in the annual reports of the foundation under the title of *The Quality of the Educational Process in the United States and in Europe*. Hopefully, Learned dispatched copies to friends of long standing. He expected prompt and thoughtful response.

In the summer of 1927 one of his close Harvard friends belatedly acknowledged receipt of "Bulletin Twenty"—after Learned had with hopeful timidity inquired about its reception. He received this reply:

I should have acknowledged before this the copy of your very interesting monograph which you were good enough to have sent to me but I was away when it arrived and have only just returned to my office. I had seen the book however, in Middlebury, Vermont where I visited President Moody for a day and I was impressed by my brief glimpse of it there and by my talk with him about it.

Learned preserved the letter among his papers with a notation from Milton to the effect that "they also serve who only stand and wait."

Late in the fall Abraham Flexner wrote a belated note to Learned in which he said: "I do not know how it happens that I did not write you on the subject of your book."

The copy of "Bulletin Twenty" sent to President A. Lawrence Lowell at Harvard went unacknowledged for more than a year. Through Dean Henry W. Holmes, of the Graduate School of Education, Learned discovered that President Lowell had sent a copy to every member of the Harvard Corporation. In a note to Holmes Learned said: "I haven't as yet heard from President Lowell . . . although I am flattered by the obvious approval that his action indicates."

Toward the end of June 1928 President Lowell acknowledged the transmission of Learned's report without any observation concerning its central thesis. Lowell said this:

I have read in the Bulletin your remarks about what I have been trying to do in Harvard College, having previously seen only a brief abstract in the newspaper; and I want to tell you what a gratification your remarks are to me. The real secret, I believe, of our appeal to the imagination of the students is that, unlike almost every other college, we have applied the system of general examinations and tutors to the whole undergraduate body instead of to an honor group. Thus the path to honors is always open, and many of those who must take the general examinations anyway are tempted to do it with distinction. They can write their thesis in the last year, and do whatever else is necessary for honors.

The response of President W. N. P. Faunce, of Brown University, was, however, immediate and enthusiastic. Speaking of "Bulletin Number Twenty," Faunce said: "I wish to use it in the reconstruction of our curriculum." The communication, however, was sent to the foundation, rather than to Learned, a Brown alumnus, with the impersonal salutation "Dear Sir." Faunce died before he had opportunity to carry out his intention.

While American higher education incorporated the Graduate Record Examination into its tradition and the apparatus of the Educational Testing Service as a part of its equipment, the educational thinking in which the examination program had its roots, deserves to be dusted off and restudied. It is the thesis of this volume that in due time William S. Learned will go down in the history of higher education as one of the few major influentials—one of the originative minds.

The span of Learned's active career encompassed the years of the great debate in higher education. During the period practically every basic policy of American higher education was explored, challenged, and resolved in a variety of way which spread across the educational spectrum. For the most part the controversy concentrated on the scrutiny of four policies namely: (1) Content: *what to teach;* (2) Method: *how to teach;* (3) Selection: *whom to admit,* and (4) *Orientation;* what outlook should be communicated. (177) Since Learned for all appearances proceeded in his studies outside the area of controversy along the avenue whose direction his own research mapped for him to travel, the character of his thinking can best be studied in the context of his times by stating his position and then showing how other educational thinking differed from him.

For purposes of this comparative analysis, Learned's thinking can be summarized around eight key concepts: (1) *intellectuality,* (2) *discovery,* (3) *continuity,* (4) *coherence,* (5) *interest with obligation,* (6) *personal relationships,* (7) *intellectual climate,* and (8) *measurement.* The concept of higher education which emerged from Learned's research and meditation required a working fusion of all eight ingredients.

Intellectuality

It was Learned's starting point that education is "intellectual." In the practical consequences of his conception of knowledge

Learned saw far-reaching philosophical implications. He proposed to hold the student responsible for the permanent and available mastery of "knowledge." That kind of knowledge, he said, must be "so familiar and so sharply defined that it comes freely to mind when needed and can be depended on as an effective cross-fertilizing element for producing fresh ideas." (178)

In the second place, Learned held that "a student's knowledge, when used as adequate evidence of education . . . should represent as nearly as possible the complete individual." It should furnish, to use Learned's phrase, "a coherent intellectual physiognomy." (179)

"The way out of educational confusion," as Learned saw the pathway, was through the reassertion of the fundamental intellectual purpose of the college. He explained his position by saying that:

> Released from genuine intellectual demands, an abounding student energy has raised a crop of general activities that have not only subordinated the main task, but to a very great extent, both in student and in public opinion, have assumed the crown of sanction for the whole process. We bewail the fact and seek to "regulate" student activities, without perceiving that if what we still believe to be the major operations were convincingly carried out, the others would of themselves fall into the proper perspective. (180)

Learned, always confident that a potential existed within the student which if once challenged and liberated might "surpass our most sanguine expectations," asserted that the failure "to capitalize the intellectual vision, energy, and enthusiasm of the young minds trying to get their bearings is appalling." (181)

Learned was unconcerned with any program for the integration of the college which did not result from the primary assertion of its intellectual purpose. He made scant reference to Chicago and President Robert M. Hutchins. He paid no attention to the progressives. He never mentioned Irving Babbitt or Norman Foerster. He proposed no way out which did not make strenuous intellectual work central. He advocated no patent educational remedies. He found no sense whatever in statements like the following by Foerster:

> If it be true, as I believe, that the mind and will of twentieth-century man are sick, it behooves us not to treat the symptoms, as the social planners propose, or ignore the disease, as the apostles of adult activities and survey courses propose, but to seek to cure the disease. That disease, I think we must agree with Irving Babbitt and President Hutchins, is chaos. Its symptoms are bewilderment, drifting, loss of standards, loss of appetite for life. . . . The remedy is adoption of a humanistic or religious working philosophy, and the cure, it may conceivably turn out, will not be complete until we have built up a metaphysics or a theology as impressive as those of ancient Greece and the Middle Ages. (182)

The reassertion of order in the college, to be achieved by restoring the primacy of "metaphysics" in the curriculum at Chicago or reintroducing a course in the study of the great books of the world, as Foerster proposed, was as alien to the thought of Learned as it was to John Dewey and Harry D. Gideonse.

Discovery

Within the framework of the intellectual purpose of the college, Learned asserted as the first duty of the institution the obligation to *know the student* as Socrates had once urged his followers to "know thyself." To him this process meant something entirely different from subjecting a "battered student," survivor of a "battery of tests" to a staff of expert advisers, as Norman Foerster observed, with an efficiency not to be outdone "by Standard Oil. Forever tested, examined, analyzed, advised, prodded, the young collegian of the Chicago plan has scant time to reflect upon his personal independence and responsibility." (183)

Learned proposed to banish the *average* student from the college by disposing of the

> machinery he has produced: the disconnected curriculum pieced together in semester installments to suit the unstudied and constantly shifting average demand; the rigidly administered courses imposing their average selection and quality on good and poor alike; the

domination of the average performance of a small group as reflected in comparative class ratings. (184)

Once the college has disposed of the "average student," the institutional emphasis reverts to the ancient tradition of individual education. "There remain only individuals." (185) Learned went on to say that

These should command exclusive attention. What they are, what they know, what they can and will learn, are separate, individual problems. When we behave officially as though all . . . students were alike we deny the student a revelation that lies at the core of all educational reality. If the educational process has any chance whatever of inducing a respect for intellectual honesty and the habit of its practice, this can result only from the truthful and realistic manner in which individual minds are dealt with. *There can be few formulas for the purpose;* more than in most other services the successful educator must depend on intelligence. (186)

Continuity

By liberating the student from the mechanical task of accumulating an arbitrary credit account, Learned proposed to confront the individual with an intellectual objective that would promote his real educational development. He protested the discontinuity in the credit-bound educational process. He explained his position by suggesting that:

Instead of making a through trip from New York to Chicago without change and with suitable stops, no traveler would profit by changing every hundred miles to an independent road with a different gauge of vehicles, different passenger regulations and a different coinage with which to negotiate transportation. Fully parallel is the mental delay and friction arising during a student's journey through the hands of fifty teachers who, instead of helping him toward a single intellectual goal that he might clearly see and aspire to reach, severely hold him up for the satisfaction of tasks devised by themselves for the purpose of appraising and rating his efforts to swell an arbitrary credit account. (187)

Learned urged a relationship between a student and "his"

professor which would provide for continuity in individual development on one intellectual expedition unbroken by timed unit intervals. Taking a pattern from the English tutor, Learned wanted to see the time come when a competent older man would be "dealing intimately and progressively with each student's mental life as a separate problem." (188) He looked upon the English tutor type as both an "accomplished scholar" and "an interesting man" with a continuity of relationships over an extended period on the basis of congenial intellectual comradeship.

Learned pointed to the 1890's as the decade in which the discontinuity of the educational process became firmly established with the inauguration of the "quarter system." He spoke with ironic bitterness of the development in these words:

An administrative genius adapted to education the principles of mass production by which two decades later an engineering innovator revolutionized the automobile industry. By dividing the year into four quarters, by dividing all knowledge into convenient quarterly bits, and by rounding off and sealing for preservation each bit with a test and a credit, a system was devised whereby, for anyone who had come up through the schools, an education, or at least a degree, became available in the form of interchangeable credit units taken in a very liberal order, at any time, for any purpose—the "universal" college course. . . .

In a summary of the principles of mass production Mr. Henry Ford indicates its fundamental characteristic: "The physical load is lifted off men and placed on machines. The recurrent mental load is shifted from men in production to men in designing." Similarly in the new educational system the mental burden need no longer be borne by the student; his only indispensable concern is to earn quarterly credits. The "designer," however, assumes a difficult obligation, and the last thirty years of American college administration have witnessed a desperate and fruitless effort to discharge it.

Believing that, consistently with the theory, not even a choice of definite ends could be prescribed, yet realizing the predicament of the inexperienced student, each college authority has undertaken to relieve him by pointing out how, in the abstract, the thing could be done. An elaborate accumulation of devices such as majors, minors, sequences, related fields, required subjects, free electives, limited electives, alternative electives, and so on, all testify to the "designer's" solicitude, by a hedge of regulations, to guide an unseeing student through various mental exercises that the experienced master considers desirable. It seems not to have occurred to him to give the student some clear conception of what he might hope ultimately to create, so that he could intelligently do the designing himself.

Our whole policy in this respect is rapidly proving itself a complicated failure; it produces graduates by the thousand, but not self-educated men and women. The principles of mass production are not applicable to human education of the highest type; the mental load, the ultimate design, must remain with the workman; only in so far as it does can the process be successful. (189)

Coherence

Like Learned, John Dewey felt that the presentation of studies "in doses and chunks of a ready-made subject-matter" contributed to intellectual passivity. (190) The fractionalizing of knowledge, he observed, "is inevitable as long as the educational mind is dominated by the notion that studies are identical with the traditional divisions of subject-matter. The fragments become first smaller cabins and then hardly more than pigeon-holes for odds and ends." (191)

Now it is important to note that although Learned lived through the decades of the emergence of general education in the vocabulary of the campus, he ignored the term. He never mentioned Meiklejohn or Irving Babbitt or Columbia or Chicago or Minnesota or progressive education or the Harvard report on *General Education in a Free Society* or Bennington or Sarah Lawrence or great books or St. John's or the American Council on Education in a context of general education discussion. He engaged in no consideration of "adjustment to society," or how "education must come to terms with industrial civilization and discover its tasks in the new age." (192) He never became mystical; his words pointed unequivocally to a specific referent which set in motion a sequential chain of intellectual activity. Learned's apparent disregard for the educational movements, vocabulary, and personalities of his times was the result neither of his lack of concern nor ignorance of what was taking place. He merely found nothing significant for the purpose of "his" line of inquiry. For his want of critical discussion with the important educational experimenters around him, he may perhaps be guilty. If he had been called upon to comment, he would have pointed out that general education is, will be, and has always been the objective of the college.

In the design of the Graduate Record Examination he accepted the principal subjects of a liberal education, not indeed as represented by the curriculum of any one institution, but as broadly conceived areas of knowledge. Hence Learned remained aloof from the controversy over what schedule of "redeeming" studies should constitute the core of a general education.

In his installation address at Amherst Meiklejohn had described the willingness of faculties to allow students to wander about the college curriculum as a characteristic expression of "intellectual agnosticism." In his experimental college at the University of Wisconsin some total of 327 students enrolled in the four classes of 1927, 1928, 1929, and 1930. The college provided a two-year program of studies in the problems of civilization. Freshmen studied the civilization of ancient Athens. Sophomores studied that of modern America. Faculty members were called "advisers." This term had thus an entirely different meaning from its context in Learned's discussion. In the spring of 1942 alumni of the experimental college convened in Chicago to honor Meiklejohn. The master gave two talks during the course of the celebration. He observed to his old students of other years that they were dealing with a "sick college in a sick society." He attributed the breakdown of contemporary culture and its colleges to the breakdown of theology. The disintegration of the "idea of God" from educational planning had brought about the disintegration of the unity of the teaching program. "The foundations of belief on which our civilization was built have been swept away," he said. (193)

Our education will not recover its unity, its sanity, until we recognize again the essential human validity of our Christian tradition. If we strip away from that tradition all elements of mythical belief, we shall find at the heart of it a moral assertion which, more and more, our Protestant-Capitalistic Individualism has denied. It is the assertion of universal human brotherhood, of the fellowship of mankind. It is that assertion which alone can restore our culture, can reconstruct our education. If we wish to escape the disintegration into which our civilization has fallen, if we wish to replace war with peace, we must set up as our common goal, not the Church Universal, but the State Universal. (194)

Meiklejohn went on to say that there is only one art to which all the activities of the college should be devoted: the art of liberating intelligence.

On its subjective side that art is concerned with the transforming of Knowledge into Intelligence. On its objective side it is concerned with the creating of Human Reasonableness, of Human Fellowship. (195)

During the Meiklejohn celebration Scott Buchanan, at the time dean of St. John's College, identified two men who had deprived "a whole generation of American youths of their heritage in the classics and the liberal arts." (196) The first was Charles W. Eliot whose introduction of the elective system in Harvard University allowed the student to study what he chose, thus fragmentizing learning. The second was John Dewey who reduced "knowledge to opinion" and made "experience, the mother of opinion," into the intellectual leader of the time. (197)

To all the academic discussion which excited higher education Learned continued to be an observant spectator. He expressed no more comment on the 1945 report of President James B. Conant's Committee on the Objectives of a General Education in a Free Society which proposed to "cultivate in the largest possible numbers of our future citizens an appreciation of both the responsibilities and the benefits which come to them because they are Americans and are free" than he did in Norman Foerster's 1933 two-year course for Iowa freshmen and sophomores to evoke a personal response from a study of human values in a few of the great books.

Learned, however, studied with special interest Conant's annual reports to the Harvard Corporation. He was interested in Conant's personal search to identify the minimal commitments required by a modern man to construct a philosophy of life if he be neither a religious dogmatist nor a materialistic atheist and in the Harvard president's search for the means of motivation to "self-education."

The year after Learned delivered the Inglis Lecture, Conant, the Sheldon Emery Professor of Organic Chemistry, had been installed as Harvard's twenty-third president. As a young man of seventeen, Conant had entered Harvard's freshman class in 1910. He presented himself for a series of voluntary examinations, clearing the way for the study of advanced chemistry in his first year and completing his undergraduate studies with the election to Phi Beta Kappa in three years. When he succeeded Lawrence Lowell as president, Conant saw that the design of the Harvard College which he inherited stood on three foundation stones: the tutorial, the general examination, and the residence house plan. Basic to the Harvard system was the tutorial plan established by Lowell in 1912. Four years later the general examination was introduced to provide a means for testing a student's grasp of his major field by going beyond bookkeeping mathematics. In much the same manner that Learned might have stated it, Conant expressed his liking for the general examination by saying that "to accomplish the ideal of self-education and to stimulate competition a goal must be found remote enough to require long-sustained effort, but not so remote as to be out of sight. The goal must be tangible and capable of measurement." It bothered Conant, however, that, despite all the educational effort Harward had set forth, students in their own vernacular were still "taking courses" rather than "studying subjects."

Learned recognized the enormous contribution to sound education which Harvard had made, but his reading of Conant's reports convinced him that Harvard had not yet found the productive intellectual combination which it sought to catalyze self-education.

Unmoved by his observations of the current educational discussions, Learned proceeded on the four basic premises, (1) that the unifying element in the curriculum is authentic intellectual work and that such performance is laborious and exacting, (2) that the experience of the best colleges had established well an acceptable pattern of fields of knowledge definitive of the liberal arts—and that these areas ought to be the areas to be examined in the Graduate Record Examination, (3) that a creative education produces an awareness of the relationships of ideas, and (4) that the mastery of permanent and available knowledge can be measured. The general acceptance of the Graduate Record Examination profile as the negotiable instrument of intellectual achievement is an index of the durability of Learned's concept.

It was Learned's position that every mind grows its own curriculum. He proposed to present the educational values of the curriculum to the student in groups of related ideas through personal contacts with good teachers. For Learned a curriculum evolves with the continuing discovery of the student.

Interest with Obligation

Learned proposed to place the student, with his unique and variable characteristics, in the full focus of attention. By skillful guidance he proposed to pilot the manner and spirit in which the student selects and deals with ideas that seem, at least to him, big enough and important enough to command his best efforts. It was the teacher's responsibility to bring into focus the student's educational aim. Learned specifically emphasized that

> the only aim that counts in self-education is the aim that actually prevails in the student's mind; and the aim that prevails, be it great or little, is never a vaguely echoed formula. Whether it be a mere diploma or a scholar's vision, it is whatever motive casts a path of light from the end in view to the student's next step and results in action. The first obligation of an institution for education, therefore, is to avoid setting up a meaningless aim or assuming that because a student is present in a class he has therefore appropriated an aim that was never his. (198)

College-directed self-education, Learned held, begins when interest is coupled with obligation. To him it involves three steps:

(1) to see clearly and in specific terms the desired goal—not the term-goal of a course but a plainly defined and substantial body of knowledge;

(2) to be free, with understanding advice, to choose the means for reaching it that one finds most direct and satisfactory;
(3) to do the reading, thinking, experimentation, and observation whereby one may arrive. (199)

Learned believed that the emotional acceptance which supports a student's defined aim produces an intellectual morale which supports his work and is contagious. He wanted the student to prepare a descriptive, topical picture of what after two, three, or four years, and from all sources, he hopes to have mastered—

a picture that will develop its parts and relationships as he proceeds until it presents a consistent intellectual structure that becomes real to him because it actually houses him and invites extension." (200)

Learned went on to explain that

so pictured, a student goal will involve certain bodies of knowledge, sometimes diverse, sometimes in close combination—fields of subject matter which must be cultivated, and on the understanding of which the institution can, if it will, reliably gauge any mind. If the student knows that comprehensive knowledge tests over such areas exist, he will look forword to being measured by them. They serve him in a twofold manner, (a) as evidence of the extent to which his intellectual equipment is accumulating, however his knowledge may later be utilized, and (b) as a survey of the still unmastered material in the field. (201)

Now Learned's concept was no sugared doctrine according to which obligation ceases when for any reason "interest" disappears. Once defined, the aim mapped an intellectual highway which the student was obligated to travel unless he had good and sufficent reason to alter his goal. Learned pointed out that:

the crux of the entire process rests in the responsibility of each individual for recognizing and appropriating that which will best fit his need as he can be brought to see it. . . . In general, it is a régime that contemplates education as a searching, informing way of life as a whole for students who have their work in clear focus and are operating under their own power. (202)

Personal Relationships

To Learned the motivation to self-education evolved out of the personal relationship between the teachers and the student. It was, as he saw it, "the unnatural pressure for course-credit instead of for ideas" that paralyzed common sense. (203) He held that a faculty could double the area of its helpfulness if it were "encouraged to use its teaching resources freely and informally as needed instead of being limited to course units." (204)

He states his position in these words:

> Let us assume that a college possesses exact and comprehensive knowledge of an entering student and from his history has worked out with him a careful provisional forecast of what he can reasonably accomplish. At present, such a statement could scarcely escape being made in terms of catalogued courses to be "passed." But a student's aim or goal, if justly stated, is unlike any such pattern, even if such a catalogue pattern were intelligible. *If his* intellectual objective fits what he is known to be, it has an integrity and emphasis that are unique, and that make a deep-lying appeal to his mind because of that fact. (205)

The significant intellectual encounter takes place, so Learned said, at the moment when the need for the personal wisdom and inspiration of teachers is most acutely felt. "It is," he emphasized,

> for the sake of personal associations that a company of scholars exists. . . . The best part of education for youth is to come in contact with stirring personalities that have had great adventures with ideas. If a young mind can recognize what these ideas mean and whither they tend, it is undeniably the greatest possible stimulus for him to catch these meanings from a living person. (206)

A teacher who proves equal to the demands of students "who are in business for themselves" finds the task of "policing" learning superseded by "the deliberate, critical verdict of the free student mind." (207) Believing that "originality, insight, and forceful thinking are elements that must be recognized and developed in the student's use of knowledge," Learned felt that the student, as he learns, must be inspired with a tolerance for the same intelligent criticism that he is learning to apply and with an idealism grounded in reality. These and similar purposes are the real reasons for the existence of a teacher, not the imparting of information as hitherto understood. (208)

He looked upon much of the information imparted in the classroom as "intellectual lumber" and then added:

Essential to construction, it has today become readily available for almost any subject in a hundred forms. The student is both designer and builder. He must procure the lumber, fit it to his needs, and incorporate it in the structure. The teacher is the consulting architect. He extends the builder's vision through criticism and example, coordinating the structure's functions and parts, and pointing out the best models. He has been too long and too often mistaken for a purveyor of the builder's supplies. (209)

Probably Christian Gauss at Princeton University came as close to being the kind of teacher Learned had in mind as a model as any other contemporary. Gauss not only stimulated students to come alive; he joined battle with them over ideas that kept minds in motion years after students had departed from the campus. As a matter of fact almost twenty years after Edmund Wilson was graduated, Gauss wrote the Princeton alumnus who remained his continuing student—the kind of comment which Learned held to be true teaching. Gauss said:

You measure the validity and significance of an age by its rate of progress toward a more or less particularized social revolt, whereas I would measure them without so definite or ultimate a *finem ad quem*, by the rate of spiritual metabolism which they beget throughout the widest possible reaches of the population. (210)

There was the kind of intellectual friction to ignite the fire of any student, as Learned liked to say, who is "in business for himself."

The Intellectual Climate

The interstimulating quality of personal relationships which Learned held indicative of a sustaining intellectual climate he found, to his way of thinking, exemplified in "the clear intellectual atmosphere" of the University of Toronto. (211) He felt that at Toronto and at Harvard and Swarthmore study had actually become "the major sport." Learned particularly liked Toronto because its performance was not the result of the existence of an honors system, but rather because of the fact that a majority of the students were "doing a definitely intellectual job." (212) He looked upon three American institutions—Toronto, Harvard, and Swarthmore—as representative of different forms of approach to the problem of "selecting the able mind and guiding its intellectual development." (213)

For Learned the significance of the University of Toronto rested in the fact that it conducted special curricula for a specially prepared and selected group of students numbering more than half its entire undergraduate attendance. These curricula were grouped about twenty-six different subjects or combinations of subjects. The courses in these subjects were laid out in an obligatory sequence and were supported in narrow options by other related requirements. There was no final comprehensive examination but rather annual examinations covering only the work of the year. Students had to pass, regardless of term work. In the Toronto experience Learned saw as the unifying force giving coherence to an education and creating its sustaining intellectual climate the serious purpose of an active mind.

Measurement

The kind of educational performance which Learned sought to encourage implied an arrangement for "dealing directly with ideas themselves rather than with mechanical symbols." (214) He felt current institutional procedure to be inadequate in the areas of mental diagnosis and the measurement of progress. He wanted an accurate survey of a student's "entire resources assembled through the planning and executive power of his own mind." (215) He asserted that the main criterion of an institution's educational philosophy lies in the convincing quality of its appeal to the student "as a complete intellectual entity." He posed this question as a standard for judging a college: "*Is it concerned exclusively with student response to what teachers have selected or desire to teach, or is the appropriate self-education of the individual student its real purpose?*" If the latter aim prevails, as Learned believed it should, then

the college will seek to make clear by every turn of administration and by all other influences within its power that while courses are intended to help, it is the student's own well-organized gain from all available sources that count; that, so far as possible, no aspects or content of an aggressive intellectual life will fail to register their sum or escape official recognition in making up this man's account with the college —an account which by definition is identical with his own fullest enrichment. (216)

While Learned was hard at work in the construction of the Graduate Record Examination, Norman Foerster, as director of the School of Letters, State University of Iowa, warned that the liberal college was threatened with extinction. It could be saved from death, he counseled, "only by a bold reform of its curriculum and faculty" in harmony with its mission. (217) Learned proposed rather *a clear sense of intellectual direction and intellectual work catalyzed in an intellectual climate by a true program of self-education.*

Because Learned secretly smarted under criticism from Teachers' College leaders, it is important to note what the Columbia specialists were thinking about. Norman Foerster said they condemned (1) bloated curriculum, (2) departmental walls, (3) insensitivity to contradiction in beliefs and practices, (4) the obsession with science, (5) the obsession with pedagogical method, (6) exaggerated utilitarianism, (7) the illiberality and aimlessness of the liberal arts college, and (8) the blindness of educators to the need of a social philosophy. (218)

Foerster suggested that the Teachers' College frontiersmen were pushing on toward some promised land, "seeking a new human pattern, a new conception of the good life, comparable with the Christian saint or the antique all-round man or the attempted fusion of the two in the Christian gentleman." (219) Foerster saw a vague emphasis on "the good life," which had to await the "radical reconstruction" of economic society. "The present pattern," said Foerster, "the economic man, is to be continued; only, it is to be socialized." (220)

Learned did not look for the improvement of higher education in the establishment of a social program, or in the fusion of the experimental method with a humanitarian urge, or in the instrumental philosophy of John Dewey or in the humanism of Irving Babbitt or in the metaphysics of Robert Hutchins. Like a dentist with his drill on "the spot" Learned pursued his staff task of identifying and implementing those conditions which best provide for the discovering and training of capable minds in order to advance personal growth and the national welfare by authentic intellectual achievement in a true program of self-education.

Twenty years expired between the publication of Learned's report on *The Student and His Knowledge* and James B. Conant's first report to interested citizens entitled *The American High School Today.* (221) The studies of both men were supported by the Carnegie Foundation for the Advancement of Teaching.

In his emphasis on intellectual work, "discovery" of the student, measurement, challenge to the academically talented students, motivation, and counseling Conant reported much in the tradition of Learned. The Carnegie grant under which Conant operated had been made to the Educational Testing Service which Learned had been instrumental in founding. In Conant's whole report, however, there is no reaffirmation of Learned's fundamental thesis that the student is of more importance than the curriculum and that the school cannot be free to deal with the child as a human being so long as it places supreme faith in its own administrative techniques. Both men, however, were one in asserting the primary intellectual function of the school.

Henry S. Pritchett in his preface to *The Quality of the Educational Process in the United States and in Europe* described the two ends of education in America as provision for (1) a more sincere and thorough intellectual training for all and (2) opportunities for the more capable adapted to draw out the best in the students. (222) This was precisely the question which concerned Conant a third of a century later when he raised the question as to whether under one roof and under the same management, it is possible for a school to fulfill satisfactorily three functions: Can a school at one and the same time provide a good general education for *all* the pupils as future citizens of a democracy, provide elective programs for the majority to develop useful skills, and educate adequately those with a talent for handling advanced academic subjects? (223)

Learned was concerned only with "those with talent" but it was his battle cry that the number of such students was much, much larger than current performance would seem to make apparent. Like Conant, however, he held that secondary education is the key to the school situation. Joined to higher education in one continuous voyage fitted to the unique characteristics of each individual youth, Learned saw in the habitual capacity for intellectual work and on-going self-education the kind of attitude which takes power from a zest for learning and supplies the intellectual skill and power necessary for the guidance of human affairs in a universe of significant values. The kind of learning Learned was interested in was available only for the competent and the worthy.

His doctrine, however, did not call for an intellectual *elite* typical of the European approach to the problem of education. Learned had in mind no imitation of European schools or any copy of any other known institution. He proposed a type of intellectual discipline, not to satisfy a few bright minds, still less to compete with European schools. He deplored the second and third rate intellectual performance that passes so generally for adequate education. Learned took the position that America was failing to create the conditions that make any more substantial education possible. Learned's main object was to do his part "*to set up a scale of values in education that will bring order into our confused ideas as to what clear and serious thinking is and can do.*" (224) He felt that the inauguration of a standard of high excellence at the top would serve as "a welcome draught of clean, fresh air." By the establishment of "a sincere curriculum administered by genuine masters in such a manner as to nourish and develop the intellectual morale always latent in good minds," Learned believed that "the attitude not only of the top fourth but of the entire student body would be completely transformed." (225)

He was frank to question whether a full-time school at present has anything to offer that is comparable "with the education afforded by regular employment when this is supplemented by efficient schooling of a simple sort either on the continuation school plan or preferably on the 'cooperative' scheme of periodic alteration." (226) More than thirty years after Learned asked the question, Conant, operating on a Carnegie grant, was frank enough to make explicit the answer which Learned inferred.

Learned summarized his position by saying that:

> Sentimentalism is the chief stock in trade of many politicians who regard the public schools as an easy fountain of honor and of some educational philosophers who fail to see that honest dealing with a child's intelligence is the basic and indispensable requisite in its education. (227)

For the sake of intellectual reality as well as for the sake of the community at large, Learned searched for a new scale of values. In a nation where educational experience was spreading over an ever-broadening democratic base, he wanted each citizen to acquire "a true vision of honest, objective human relationships." (228) Learned loathed the "patchword mind" which he defined as

> a brain whose thoughts are waves of semester length, whose conception of knowledge is of something to be swiftly crammed and deposited in unrelated packages, and whose experience with ideas that may be pondered, that grow luminous and tax the full intelligence for expression, is gained almost wholly, if at all, outside the classroom, partly perhaps in private activities with which restless souls have sought to supplement the kaleidoscopic and shallow operation of the official program. (229)

Conant long since has declared that the pursuit of the goal of a unified, coherent culture suitable for a nuclear age of machines and experts must place the educational process at the heart of the existence of democracy. Citizens, he has said, must pay attention to their schools, hold a true reverence for learning in the community, and see to it that future generations have a high regard for the activities of the human mind.

Long before the age of competitive atomic weaponry and the ascent of the Sputniks, Learned was pioneering the model of a new type of education which would make explicit "a definition of intellectual values with which we are willing to stand before the world." (230) The "independent" scholar of 522 Fifth Avenue devoted a single-minded and well-financed foundation life to encouraging the creation of conditions favorable to the development of institutional practices designed to encourage education as a personal matter of quantitative performance capable of objective and comparative qualitative measurement.

9

THE EXPLORATION OF APPLICATIONS

Toward an Administrative and Faculty Agenda

From the time of the publication of *The Oberlehrer* in 1914, Learned located the responsibility for the creation of an academic climate conducive to *teaching for self-education* upon the shoulders of a professionally alert faculty aware of its mission. For him the teacher, individually and as a class, stood as the key to the kind of substantial and unequivocal educational process which he championed. In lieu of a fixed external curriculum, he looked upon the instructor as a catalyst motivating the student to a concern for what is worth learning.

This position had little in common with the cafeteria election system of Charles W. Eliot of Harvard, except for the common denominator of truth which they both asserted: that a student's will to learn must come from an inner motivation. Learned was proposing no educational binge to enable freewheeling students to gravitate into snap courses. Rather, he was advocating a strenuous intellectual experience stimulated through a close human relationship between a mature and understanding teacher and a student who respects the relationship. Learned believed that genuine education looks to the mastery of knowledge and its organization into trunk-line ideas which carry a subject. He proposed to liberate the teacher from the disconcerting task of always "just getting acquainted" with the student and seeing him pass on at the end of the semester. He wanted to provide for a persistent and durable relationship. To him a genuine teacher is always systematically at work to encourage the mental growth of individual students. One of the qualities in the kind of teacher he praised was "intuitive sympathy with other minds." (231) A real teacher who has roots in the profession knows, said Learned, that his chief business is "to understand and nourish young minds." (232)

Learned was under no illusion as to the difficulty which an educator would experience in his effort to weed out the artificial habits and relations which now impede genuine education. He explained that

> it is incomparably more difficult to study individual minds and then to devise appropriate ways of aiding them in long-range attainment, than it is to give uniform treatment to human units which appear and disappear so rapidly that responsibility for real progress is lost in a maze of administration. But with all its difficulties, *it is the desire and ability thus to deal faithfully with each pupil that distinguishes the real teacher from the security-seeking place holder.* (233)

As the policies and techniques of "responsible education" become familiar to teachers, Learned believed that faculties would see their best dreams realized in an increasing number of cases and in finer outcomes.

William Learned spoke from a position of acknowledged authority about concepts statistically examined in the most massive and trustworthy survey of academic performance produced by higher education up to the time of his retirement. In substance, he said to administrative officers and faculties:

> Here are some fresh educational ideas that have emerged from our Carnegie research. Think about them. Try them. See what will happen on your campus if you have the will and courage to move from the outmoded patterns of higher education to models suitable for the modern world.

Learned wished with all his heart that some educator would try the whole program. When he felt for a moment that President Faunce at Brown University, his alma mater, might be the Christopher Columbus, he was elated. The tools which Learned forged have become as much a part of the educational process of the 1960's as nuclear fusion and space stations have in contemporary science. The structure which he hoped would be reared to sustain the program, however, remains yet to be designed.

It is precisely for this reason that a discussion of Learned's concepts will provide a robust diet in any faculty session. Made a systematic part of the continuing agenda of a series of faculty meetings, their consideration would lift routine sessions out of the academic rut and provide fodder for spirited debate and exploration. By patient discussion, which is always a condition of emotional acceptance, any faculty could invigorate its whole corporate existence and recharge the battery of its educational ideals. As a consensus of understanding might emerge, task forces could be formed to examine specific implications. Probably the time is very ripe for such a consideration. Learned once dryly pointed out that every human institution presses primarily for self-perpetuation, ease, and security of administration, the recognition and enjoyment of vested interests, and away from aggressive concern with its true function. William Learned proposed to implement "college-directed self-education." (234) He identified the chief operating problem of the college as the adaptation of its facilities and instruction in such a way as to free the powers and enhance the MOTIVATION of the student whom it has done its best to understand.

The need for the cool fresh breezes of an invigorating agenda becomes evident from the reading of the minutes of many a faculty meeting. Educational ideas all too frequently are absent from the discussion. Here is a call for a meeting of a faculty in a well-known college administered by a dean of national reputation.

MEMORANDUM

From: The Dean

To: The Faculty

SUBJECT: Call for meeting of the Faculty

The Faculty is requested to meet at 3:30 p.m., Thursday. This will be a regular session. An effort will be made to circulate a supplementary memorandum in advance of the meeting. There are few items at hand to be presented.

The minutes of a faculty meeting too often are worth reading to emphasize the absence of healthy educational considerations. Take an example:

MINUTES OF THE FACULTY

Improvement by Degrees: The Dean opened the meeting by reading a brief report to show estimates that before 1980 U. S. college enrollment may hit 5 million; that is, enrollment will double in the next 20 or 25 years. As this increase moves along, it will of course bring some increase in advanced degrees; but will that increase be sufficient to provide an adequate number of teachers?

Mardi gras holiday: Miss A. and Miss B., representing the Mardi gras Committee, presented a request to the faculty that classes be cancelled on Friday of Mardi gras Week as well as on Thursday, in order that the Mardi gras Field Day could be held on Friday morning. After some discussion, Mr. C. moved that the question be referred to the Administration Committee for study as a matter of policy, and then referred back to the faculty for action at the next meeting. Mr. C. accepted Mr. D.'s suggestion that policy regarding Freshman Skip Day be included in the motion. The motion was seconded and carried.

FCAS–Mr. F.: Mr. E. (registrar and faculty secretary) moved that the recommendation of the Committee on Academic Standing that Mr. F. be certified as having completed requirements and recommended for graduation in June be approved. Motion seconded and carried.

FCAS–9-point scale: Mr. E. moved that the recommendation of the Committee on Academic Standing that the nine-point scale for computing grade averages be officially adopted be approved. Motion seconded and carried.

FCAS–Mid-term grades: Mr. E. moved that the faculty confirm the recommendation of the Committee on Academic Standing that mid-term grades be reported to the registrar for only those students whose work is below C-minus; it being understood that it may be necessary to ask for other grades for students on probation or being considered for probation, on an individual basis. Motion seconded and carried.

FCAS–Mr. G.: The Dean informed the faculty of the action of the Committee on Academic Standing readmitting G. to the college. He will be required to sign a statement that he fully understands the requirements he must meet for graduation.

Dress in library: Mr. H. moved that the recommendation of the Joint Committee (trustees, faculty, students) that the rule regarding dress in the library and dining hall be modified, permitting Bermuda shorts to be worn in the dining hall on Saturday and Sunday evenings, be accepted. The motion was seconded and carried 32 to 12.

Noise in library: Mr. I. presented to the faculty the problem caused by socializing and related disturbances in the library, mainly on Sunday evenings, and on Monday evenings following Student Council, as it had been discussed in a meeting of the joint Faculty and Student Library Committees. The Student Council is to give further consideration to the problem in their meeting Thursday evening, October 27. Recommended suggestions for improving the situation involve publicizing the problem by a student newspaper report of Student Council, Library Committee, and faculty conclusions; about five minutes of class time given by each member of the faculty to a presentation of the problem; and investigation of the possibility of opening the Student Center on Sunday evenings. Policing the library as a possible solution is not considered desirable. After considerable discussion of the problem, it was agreed that Mr. I. will discuss the possibility of opening the center on Sunday evenings with the business manager; and will write a statement to be used by the faculty for presenting the problem in their classes.
It was moved and seconded that the meeting adjourn. The motion was lost.

Baccalaureate: Mr. J. moved that discussion of attendance at Baccalaureate be postponed until the next meeting in order to give the seniors an opportunity to consider the problem. The motion was seconded and carried. Mr. J. moved that between now and the next meeting the president confer with the officers of the senior class or with the entire class on attendance at Baccalaureate and report to the next faculty meeting. Motion seconded and carried.

Schedule: Proposed class schedule changes brought before the faculty were read. No action was taken.

Convocations: No action was taken on the matter of student attendance at convocations.

Vanderbilt Essay: Mr. K. announced the Vanderbilt Essay Contest and asked for faculty cooperation.

Mrs. L. asked that full names be used in addressing campus mail to Mrs. Dean and Mr. Dean to avoid confusion in the post office.

Golf: Mr. I. announced a proposed faculty golf tournament. Interested faculty should contact Mr. J., Mr. M., or Mr. N.

Fellowships: Announcements regarding fellowships, grants, etc., available either to students or to faculty may be sent to the library. They will be placed on a table in the Browsing Room.
The faculty adjourned at 5:40 p.m.

Secretary of the Faculty

(Please report any corrections in writing to the secretary.)

It will become apparent to many administrators and faculty members from a careful reading of minutes that a tonic of the kind prescribed by William Learned might provide an invigorating elixir to tone up the whole academic performance. Indeed, Learned modestly pointed out that many of his suggestions referred to well-known practices long since tried out in various institutions that have successfully attacked the problem.

While every faculty would have to shape its own systematic agenda for a discussion of Learned's ideas to suit its own folkways, it may be helpful to suggest the kind of topics which may prove helpful. Of course the first step would be to provide a memorandum giving an overview of Learned's work as preliminary orientation to his concepts. If, after discussion of Learned's general approach, a faculty should act favorably on the suggestion for a further and critical review of them, the chapters of this book might become agenda units at successive meetings. There should be no haste in scheduling and no desire to "get through" with the work. Educational thinking must have time to take root and grow. The series of discussions might be a part of the regular faculty meeting or provided for in a voluntary faculty seminar. In any case the series might be begun with an earnest consideration of the full meaning of student-accepted responsibility for self-education. What does such a concept imply in the character of relationships between teacher and student? What is the implication curriculum-wise? What does the process require in the nature of cumulative information about each student? What would it mean in terms of examination policy, measurement, and evaluation?

Once the Learned concept is understood in general terms, the faculty might review the college policy from student admission to graduation. No educational therapy could be undertaken equal to a review of admissions policies by a whole faculty. A scrutiny of the process by which an annual complement of students is provided as an entering class will provide amazing information! Few professors are aware of the operations by which prospective students are actually identified, interviewed, and persuaded to enroll yet every college from the Ivy League down is intensively competitive. In the best operations the contest is to get the best brains; in others the best brawn or a distribution of special talent.

Suppose recruiting and interviewing officers should sit down with the whole faculty and describe exactly how they perform their jobs. How do they get their leads? What literature do they distribute? How do they explain the college program? What are the persuasive propositions in the "sales" talk by which the prospective student is brought to sign an application and pay the fee? A forthright discussion of the technique would prove to be mutually beneficial to the faculty and the recruiters.

A next topic might be an examination of the depth and duration of the relationships between the college and the secondary schools from which the student body is recruited. To what extent does the admissions policy of the college provide for continuous intellectual voyage and present worth? How is information about the students communicated to faculty members? How is such information—if it is communicated at all—used in the guidance and placement of students? What has been the experience of the college with the Advanced Placement Program operated in the interests of able students? How effective has this program been as an instrument of cooperation between secondary schools and the college? What experiences are these able students having with the teachers and curriculum at the level of their major interests?

William Learned would have rejoiced in the description of the Advanced Placement Program, administered by the Educational Testing Service which was the realization of his dream; for its theory speaks his idiom. The program "provides challenging experiences" for able secondary school teachers *and* able students. It encourages schools and colleges to "think of students as individuals." It directs attention to subject matter and to the teaching of this subject matter. It stimulates "creative curricular thinking" and "curricular flexibility." It provides a harness by means of which schools and colleges work together in an effective way. By placing students in work according to their measured ability, it broadens and deepens educational experience.

Is there merit in Learned's proposal for a preceptorial semester? What would the introduction of such a plan mean in terms of personnel, budget, leadership? How would such an innovation affect existing orientation programs? What would it mean for Greek-letter rushing? The mere proposal of a wholly academic first semester disturbs the whole existing routine and requires rethinking of the entire folkways of the campus. Whether the idea should prove feasible or not, its examination in the context of possible utilization would place many existing programs in a new light.

What would happen further if the whole academic strait jacket invented to provide for breadth and depth in education should be discarded in favor of a curriculum shaped to reflect the individual abilities, the personal goals, and the inner motivations of the student? What outcomes might be expected if mature and responsible professors, dealing face to face with students whom they know intimately, should replace the registrar as the final authority in the determination of the pattern of an individual's education? Learned had no misgivings whatsoever about what would happen. He believed that genuine education would take root. But the transformation would inevitably be accomplished by a shifting in the center of gravity from "the professional faculty committeemen who know all the rules as Hoyle would have them" to those mature members of the faculty who know what genuine education really means.

Take another example. What would happen on a campus if the library was put under scrutiny in the light of Learned's concepts of self-education? What members of the library staff deal regularly with students? Do the members of the library staff in their private offices and workrooms constitute a professionally more competent group than the personnel regularly assigned to work with students? Are functionally competent librarians available to think intellectual problems through with students as they search among the stacks for ideas that at the moment have living power? What do faculty minutes show about library activities as a part of the genuine educational problem?

Again, what of all the elaborate apparatus to police "the mark"? What would an examination policy incorporating the Learned concept involve in academic organization, expense, and time? Would it be helpful to faculty and students to draft memorandums describing fields of knowledge to give students a motivating vision of what the area is all about? Suppose, in the Learned pattern, the faculty as a whole should undertake the rewriting of the whole catalogue? Imagine a catalogue written to describe an academic program rather than one which is altered only in calendar dates and academic vital statistics?

Realism in American education, Learned forecast, will come about through a "simple but drastic revolution" which restores to education "the sense of achievement in its own terms" defined as the mastery of important knowledge. It will be advanced by the "systematic, unremitting study and recorded analysis" of the student to provide for a thorough understanding of the texture, strength, and bearing capacity of each growing mind. It will use this knowledge, "not in fitting the candidate to a curriculum, but in aiding him, through his own native drive and selective skill, to construct his own curriculum of earned and tested ideas in whose company he can live and grow with satisfaction to himself and with profit to society." And finally, the new pattern in its coherence would provide for the identification and measurement of primary educational values. (235)

In discussing Learned a distinguished educator asked this question:

> Why did Learned sound like a progressive when he talked about self-direction and like Hutchins when he talked about intellectual achievement? How did his ideas compare with some of the notable experiments in college education of his day—Meiklejohn's Experimental College, Aydellotte's honor system, Bennington, etc., etc.? Did the Depression and the New Deal have no effect whatever upon his views of college education?

The answer to these questions is that the times had no more influence upon Learned, as far as the lines of his inquiry were concerned, than Martin Luther did upon the works of Nicolaus Copernicus. With the exception of the Swarthmore experience, Learned discussed few of these topics directly or by inference. He was not an eclectic. For more than thirty years he pursued a fundamental line of research. The tools which he helped to design have become the accepted coin of the educational world of the 1960's. Will it not perhaps be profitable to retrace his educational pilgrimage and see how a faculty *and* a student body involved too in the discussion, might react to the whole message? Learned formulated the question in issue. He said:

> Not that every pupil would become a scholar under any regime, but the school that centers its steady emphasis on the real core of the process, namely, understanding, . . . has one incomparable advantage: it uses all the power it has and can arouse in the pupil in the only right direction; the pupil will never make the ugly and desolating discovery that what was all-important for graduation suddenly has no importance for life. (236)

10

THE DURABILITY OF THE CONCEPTS

Structural Influence in American Education

While Learned's position in the development of American education will ultimately be determined at the campus level by the acceptance of the therapeutic ideas which he advocated, his considerable influence can already be defined. What has been the impact of his performance? Does a restudy of his inquiries and meditations light a path which leads in a direction of value to the 1960's? Does Learned deserve renewed attention from a generation of educators now unfamiliar with his name, with the nature of his proposals, with the history of important ideas and tools which have become as habitual in everyday academic use as the hammer and saw in the hands of the carpenter?

The answer to these questions can best begin with a restatement of his major premise: *The pursuit of authentic intellectual goals is education's only valid task.* He wanted to throw overboard the "initial falsehood in terms of which the social and administrative aim in education is now expressed and executed." (237) With the acid clarity characteristic of his speech, Learned proposed to substitute "the independent, demonstrable mastery of ideas" of the student's ultimate design for the "factitious obligation to keep abreast of a time schedule." (238) So unquenchable was his faith that such a change would redeem the wasted intellectual resources lying untapped within potentially capable students that he believed an inversion of "the System" would produce a wholesome response. Statistically he was confident that he was right.

Contemporary voices, it needs to be noted, are once again raising the issues which so seriously concerned the "Scholar of 522 Fifth Avenue" and doing so under more urgent circumstances. In *The House of the Intellect*, for example, Jacques Barzun observes that "the lack of clear notions and express demands produces the same effect as incompetence and dishonesty." He points out that "the very customs of the academic grove militate against standards. The system of credits turns attention away from substance. The student amasses points in order to advance, as in the game of parchesi." (239) And again: "Education with us has managed to reconcile the contradictory extremes of being a duty and a diversion, and to elude intellectual control so completely that it can become an empty ritual without arousing protest." (240)

Much the same position is inferred in the statement of national goals for strengthening science and engineering developed by the President's Science Advisory Committee. (241) The Eisenhower report urges more attention to adapting educational programs to the varying competence of students. Especially it asks for more attention to the needs of the gifted, "greater devotion to learning, and a greater pride in intellectual achievement." Four primary considerations in the report identify the very issues which Learned held to be paramount, namely, attention to (1) the curriculum and content of courses; (2) the quality and effectiveness of teachers; (3) the recognition and encouragement of promising students; and (4) the development of intellectual leadership.

The specific language of the report is so much in the Learned idiom that one might easily believe that the text had been written by the "Scholar of 522 Fifth Avenue" at least a dozen years before the ascent of Sputnik. I. Here is a verbatim record of the committee's summary:

> We therefore conclude that Americans should attach greater value to intellectual excellence.

Every school and college should re-examine its curriculum to make sure that in every respect it is giving adequate challenge to the intellectual capacities of its students.

We should do far more than we are now doing to enhance the prestige of the teacher and to provide him with more effective support in his efforts to improve the effectiveness of his teaching.

We should move much further in the direction of adapting our educational programs to the widely varying competence of students, and seek especially to meet the needs of the most gifted students.

"All worthy objectives!" Learned would have said dryly. "And how?"

The fact needs to be recorded that, important as was the scientific and engineering performance of the Russians in shooting the Sputniks into orbit in October and November 1957, the general discussion came into focus around the effect of the achievement upon the competitive power positions of the United States and the Soviet Union. In the end the topic was not science and engineering but rather the comparative quality of American and Communist education. A content analysis of *The Wall Street Journal* during the Sputnik months shows that the major discussions in this sophisticated newspaper centered around the relative superiority of the schools. While solutions soon looked to Washington for more financial aid, the study indicates a businessman's concern with three topics: (1) the need to revise the curriculum; (2) the need for more administrative ingenuity in maximizing resources; and (3) the need for more effective use of talent among teachers and students. (242) It became apparent, educationally speaking, that it was "time for a change." Learned anticipated the panic; he questioned the power of any educational system not rooted in authentic intellectual performance.

Within a decade after his death dramatic events in outer space were vividly confronting American education with issues which he had defined as critical from the publication of his first study of *The Oberlehrer*. In the perspective of developments, it is clear that William Learned put this finger on the right problem and asked the right question. Merely to ask the right question, as Irving Babbitt once observed, is a distinction of no small order.

Learned advocated reform which would maximize the cooperation of the institution with the student in the achievement of his aim. The institution's valid task, Learned insisted, is to plumb and unlock the capacities of the student, one by one, so that he can master "ideas to the point of grasping their essential relations." (243) By objective and dramatic evidence Learned in his day confronted educational leaders with the proof that the phrase "individual differences" is not a trivial concept of concern only to professional psychologists. Rather, *the idea represents the most important single fact with which teachers and educational administrators have to deal.* To Learned the concept was the point of departure in effective teaching.

Ben Wood gives it as his opinion that "not one in ten thousand college presidents and professors in the 1920's had the vaguest notion of the extent and frequency of differences within their own graduating classes until they were slapped in the face by some of the earliest charts and tables later included in *The Student and His Knowledge.*" (244) Before Learned's Pennsylvania study there had been evidence that education was going to have to come to grips with the factor of individual differences. It required the reputation of Learned and the weight of his Carnegie connections, however, to give a color of respectability to the subject. Ben Wood's study, which appeared as Volume I of the extensive report of the Modern Foreign Language Study in 1927, had been dismissed by educational leaders of the 1920's as coming from an "unknown," "unseasoned," and "brash" young man in his early 30's!

Under the imprint and authority of the Carnegie Foundation, nevertheless, the revelations about individual differences shocked and awakened the educational public. The late Professor Charles Judd, University of Chicago, enraged by the whole Learned thesis, urged his followers to publish scathing denunciations of the Pennsylvania study and all its impudent insinuations against "American education, which, as everyone knows, is the best in the world." At the time when the Learned studies were pyramiding proof, the college and its curriculum, as Ben Wood says, "were sacred cows whose holiness only hopeless heretics and enemies of the people could question."

The corollary of individual differences of course is individualized education. In the face of findings which pointed to the crying need for fitting education to the needs of the student as an individual, Learned suggested practical implementing steps. The mechanics developed for the task of individualizing education exist today at every hand: testing programs which have become feasible for even the poorest institutions; mechanical, electric, electronic, and transistorized machines for scoring; statistical and analytical apparatus; cumulative records containing information about students considered as individuals; and improved methods of collecting, recording, interpreting, and using such information for maximum development of each student as an individual in society. Behind the development of the gadgetry produced to undergird the movement, however, there lay the body of motivating ideas and new purposes, the body of theory pointing to better teaching for self-education as a life goal.

The importance of Learned's outlook as a *modus operandi* becomes apparent now in a broader field from the findings in a study issued by the American Council on Education under grants from the Calkins and Ford foundations. In an exploration of *The College Influence on Student Character* (245) analysts explored relationships between intellectual training and character influence. Out of this study emerged a concept called "the level of expectancy." Such a concept was implicit in all of Learned's work. In student vernacular the idea may be expressed like this: "Oh sure, I've received good marks and all that, but I've never really had to work very hard. Now that it's almost over I feel as though I've been cheating myself, or maybe I've been cheated. I've never really been pushed." (246)

The educational experts involved in the study reported in their idiom that "our experiences with students and faculty members suggest that expectations are best established by starting with the student where he is (and that will vary widely) and encouraging him to perform to the outer limits of his capacity (which also will have wide variations)." (247)

The American Council on Education study specifically points out that "the success of any character development emphasis rests first on the *level of expectancy*. The college *can* expect more of its students." (248) Indeed the study takes the further position that "the college's best contribution to character is a direct product of the proper, balanced emphasis on learning. To contribute to character, the environment must reflect this commitment to learning as the *raison d'être* of all that happens on the college campus and to the college student." (249) In summary the report says: "We have reached what to us is a major conclusion: that *the college's unique and best contribution to character is a direct product of a properly balanced emphasis on learning.*" (250) Then it adds:

> Out of this study we conclude further that, if the college is to seek a larger role in the lives of its students, it is obligated to make a greater effort to break from tradition in both form and substance. It has been discouraging to us to see, for instance, how often the present rigidity of the college reduces its potentialities. Further experimentation obviously is desirable. . . . We feel this so strongly that we take perhaps the usual position that we need less attention henceforth to studies of the student and much greater attention to positive efforts to meet his needs. . . . Dissatisfaction with the marking and credit system, for instance, will never be mitigated until something better emerges out of a number of trials and errors. (251)

Reading that passage on a summer day at his Boothbay Harbor *Sprucewold* retreat, Learned would have smiled and observed: "And now we're in the 1960's!"

While the American Council study is careful to point out that "the development of character as well as intellect in the college is the result of no single influence or set of experiences," it does identify six elements for particular attention, namely (1) the level of expectancy, (2) the effect of environment, (3) the concept of teaching, (4) the organization of the curriculum, (5) the degree of student responsibility, and (6) the opportunity for religious understanding and practice. (252) Central in the thesis of *The College Influence on Student Character* stand the two implied factors of "discovery" and "cooperation" in the relationship between an enlightened teacher and a student awakened to the quest.

Although Learned made no effort to relate his concern for authentic intellectual goals to character education, he did observe that "the system is the same whether virtue or knowledge is at stake." (253) There is reason to believe from emerging evidence that Learned's idea of responsible education is quite as necessary to authentic moral growth as to genuine intellectual achievement.

The Educational Testing Service of course stands as a major monument to Learned's vision. ETS, established in December 1947 as a result of negotiations initiated by Learned between the American Council on Education, the College Entrance Examination Board, and the Carnegie Foundation for the Advancement of Teaching, operates as a nonprofit, independent agency with headquarters located in Princeton, New Jersey.

On a wooded 340 acre site on Rosedale Road, four miles from the center, three new functional buildings provide working space for some 500 permanent employees, augmented during test periods by some 400 additional personnel.

In a single year ETS provides examinations for nearly a million candidates. Through the Cooperative Test Division it distributes more than 8,000,000 answer sheets for tests published by it. Gross income from operations exceeds $6,000,000 a year, with substantial funds being allocated to educational research and fellowships. ETS has realized Learned's dream: it serves as *a technical and research center to provide a common denominator of educational measurements and information to enable teachers better to individualize instruction and objectively determine how students deal with ideas.*

Pursuant to the Education Act of 1958, provision has been made to extend grants-in-aid to the several states to strengthen their testing and guidance programs. At a moment in history when means for identifying the capacities and achievements of all students has become a necessity, the Educational Testing Service, thanks to the foresight of Learned and his associates of the 1940's, exists as the most unique educational agency in the world, implementing the individualizing concept of education.

In his Inglis Lecture Learned had suggested the outlines of an educational policy. "We must," he said, "make it our business to deal with the best education we know in its own terms, taking full account not only of our varied social aims but also of *the many-sided integrity of the growing mind.*" (254) In his first memorandum written from Germany to the Carnegie Foundation for the Advancement of Teaching, he had expressed the opinion that "we ought always to keep clear the way in our institutions of higher learning for capable minds of every condition of life to rise from the bottom to the top." (255) Nevertheless, he felt that education is "in the highest degree" selective; its obligation is to select those who can learn and desire to do so. (256)

To the 1960's Learned would counsel five courses of action. *First,* simplify the curriculum. *Second,* enrich the teacher. *Third,* banish the instructor who polices the assimilation of a textbook. *Fourth,* develop the college as an agency to attend, supply, and encourage students who are using their own minds. *Fifth,* find pleasure in the intellectual life.

Using these concepts for analysis, one can identify the durable influences of the "Scholar of 522 Fifth Avenue" wherever they exist by asking five other questions: Is there sincerity and directness of aim? Is there thorough discovery of the student? Is there cooperation toward an individual and self-sought goal? Is there honest, objective appraisal of results? If so, Carnegie's staff radical would agree that an educational situation exists where "teaching is for self-education as a life goal."

Notes

1. *The Quality of the Educational Process in the United States and Europe*, p. 105.
2. *Ibid.*, p. 36.
3. First published in the *Educational Review* (April 1911), pp. 345–370, and reprinted by the foundation.
4. *An Experiment in Responsible Learning*, p. 5.
5. *The Student and His Knowledge*, p. 44.
6. *Realism in American Education*, pp. 50–51.
7. *The Oberlehrer*. Cambridge: Harvard University Press, 1914. P. 150.
8. *Ibid.*, p. 123.
9. *Ibid.*, p. ix.
10. *An American Teacher's Year in a Prussian Gymnasium*, p. 367.
11. *The Professional Preparation of Teachers for American Public Schools*, p. xviii.
12. *Ibid.*, p. 8.
13. *Ibid.*, p. 9.
14. *Ibid.*
15. *The American Public Library and the Diffusion of Knowledge*, p. 56.
16. *Ibid.*, p. 70.
17. *Ibid.*, p. 66.
18. *Ibid.*, p. 70.
19. *The Quality of the Educational Process in the United States and Europe*, p. ix.
20. *Ibid.*, p. 6.
21. *Ibid.*, p. 35.
22. *Ibid.*, p. 36.
23. *Ibid.*, pp. 36–37.
24. *Ibid.*, p. 44.
25. *Realism in American Education*, p. 29.
26. *Ibid.*, p. 9.
27. *Ibid.*, pp. 46–48.
28. *Admission to College*, p. 34.
29. *Ibid.*, pp. 34–35.
30. *Realism in American Education*, p. 28.
31. *Two Decades of Educational Enquiry*.
32. *Ibid.*, p. 26.
33. *Ibid.*, p. 27.
34. *Ibid.*, pp. 27–28.
35. *Ibid.*, p. 28.
36. *Ibid.*
37. *Ibid.*, pp. 28–31.

38. *Ibid.*, p. 29.
39. *Ibid.*
40. *Ibid.*
41. *Ibid.*
42. *Ibid.*
43. *Ibid.*, p. 31.
44. *Ibid.*
45. *Ibid.*
46. *Ibid.*, p. 32.
47. *Ibid.*
48. *Ibid.*, pp. 32–33.
49. *Ibid.*, p. 33.
50. *Ibid.*
51. *Ibid.*, pp. 33–34.
52. *Ibid.*, p. 34.
53. *Ibid.*
54. *Ibid.*
55. *Ibid.*, p. 35.
56. *Ibid.*
57. *Ibid.*, p. 36.
58. *Ibid.*, p. 37.
59. *Ibid.*, p. 37.
60. *Ibid.*
61. *Ibid.*, p. 38.
62. *Ibid.*
63. *Ibid.*
64. *Ibid.*
65. *Ibid.*, p. 39.
66. *Ibid.*
67. *Ibid.*
68. *Ibid.*, pp. 39–40.
69. *Ibid.*, p. 40.
70. *Ibid.*, pp. 40–41.
71. *Ibid.*, pp. 41–42.
72. *Ibid.*, p. 42.
73. *Ibid.*, p. 43.
74. *Ibid.*
75. *Ibid.*
76. *Ibid.*, p. 44.
77. *Ibid.*, p. 44.
78. *Ibid.*, pp. 44–45.
79. *Ibid.*, p. 45.
80. *Ibid.*
81. *Ibid.*
82. *Ibid.*, p. 46.
83. *Ibid.*
84. *Ibid.*, p. 47.
85. *Admission to College*, p. 23.
86. *Ibid.*, p. 24.
87. *Ibid.*, p. 24.

88. *Ibid.*, pp. 24–25.
89. *Ibid.*, p. 25.
90. *Ibid.*, p. 26.
91. *Ibid.*, p. 27.
92. *Ibid.*, p. 28.
93. *Ibid.*, p. 31.
94. *Ibid.*
95. *Ibid.*, p. 32.
96. *Ibid.*, p. 33.
97. *Ibid.*, p. 34.
98. *Ibid.*, pp. 34–35.
99. *Ibid.*, p. 35.
100. *Ibid.*
101. *Ibid.*, pp. 36–37.
102. *Ibid.*, p. 41.
103. *Ibid.*
104. *Ibid.*, p. 42.
105. *Ibid.*, p. 43.
106. *Ibid.*
107. *Educational Testing Service general statement release.*
108. *Realism in American Education*, p. 35.
109. *Ibid.*, pp. 65–66.
110. *The College and the Freshman*, p. 4.
111. *Ibid.*, p. 6.
112. *Ibid.*
113. *Ibid.*, p. 7.
114. *Ibid.*, p. 16.
115. *Ibid.*, p. 17.
116. *Ibid.*
117. *Ibid.*, p. 18.
118. *Ibid.*, p. 20.
119. *Ibid.*, p. 21.
120. *Ibid.*, p. 22.
121. *Ibid.*, pp. 22–23.
122. *Ibid.*, p. 23.
123. *Ibid.*
124. *Ibid.*, p. 24.
125. *Ibid.*
126. *Ibid.*, p. 25.
127. *Ibid.*, pp. 25–26.
128. *Ibid.*, p. 26.
129. *Ibid.*, pp. 26–27.
130. *Ibid.*, p. 27.
131. *Ibid.*
132. *Ibid.*, p. 28.
133. *Ibid.*
134. *Ibid.*, p. 29.
135. *Ibid.*
136. *Ibid.*, p. 30.
137. *Ibid.*

138. *Ibid.*, pp. 30–31.
139. *Ibid.*, p. 31.
140. *Ibid.*
141. *Ibid.*, pp. 31–32.
142. *Ibid.*, p. 33.
143. *The Student and His Knowledge*, pp. xii–xiii.
144. *Realism in American Education*, pp. 13–14.
145. *Ibid.*, p. 17.
146. *Ibid.*, p. 18.
147. *Ibid.*, p. 19.
148. *Ibid.*, pp. 19–20.
149. *Ibid.*, p. 12.
150. *Ibid.*, pp. 24–25.
151. *Ibid.*, p. 36.
152. *Ibid.*, pp. 36–37.
153. *What's in a "Mark,"* p. 36.
154. *An Experiment in Responsible Learning*, p. 12.
155. *Ibid.*
156. *Ibid.*, p. 13.
157. *Ibid.*
158. *Ibid.*, p. 14.
159. *Ibid.*
160. *Realism in American Education*, p. 62.
161. *Ibid.*, p. 52.
162. *Ibid.*, p. 60.
163. *Ibid.*, p. 49.
164. Letter from Ben Wood, January 6, 1959.
165. Unpublished manuscript of address before the Associated Colleges and Universities of the state of New York, October 7, 1939.
166. *Ibid.*
167. *An Experiment in Responsible Learning*, p. 8.
168. *Ibid.*
169. *The College and the Freshman*, p. 6.
170. *Cases Illustrating Its Use for the Admission and Adjustment of Returning Service Men and Women*, p. 2.
171. *The Way Out of Educational Confusion*, p. 1.
172. *Universities: American, English, German.* New York: Oxford University Press, 1930, p. 213.
173. *The Higher Learning in a Democracy.* New York: Farrar & Rinehart, Inc., 1937, p. 1.
174. *Learning and Living:* Proceedings of an Anniversary Celebration in Honor of Alexander Meiklejohn. Chicago: Walker H. Hill, 1942, p. 16.
175. *The Student and His Knowledge*, p. 5.
176. *The Quality of the Educational Process in the United States and Europe*, p. 6.
177. For a discussion, see Mowat G. Fraser, *The College of the Future:* An Appraisal of Fundamental Plans and Trends in American Higher Education. New York: Columbia University Press, 1937, p. 529.
178. *The Student and His Knowledge*, p. 7.
179. *Ibid.*, p. 8.

180. *The Quality of the Educational Process in the United States and in Europe*, p. 4.
181. *Ibid.*, pp. 118–119.
182. Norman Foerster, *The Future of the Liberal College*. New York: D. Appleton-Century Company, 1938, p. 73.
183. *Ibid.*, p. 52.
184. *The Student and His Knowledge*, p. 45.
185. *Ibid.*
186. *Ibid.*
187. *The Quality of the Educational Process in the United States and in Europe*, p. 45.
188. *Ibid.*, p. 85.
189. *Ibid.*, pp. 103–104.
190. *The Way Out of Educational Confusion*, p. 34.
191. *Ibid.*, p. 14.
192. George S. Counts, *Secondary Education and Industrialism*, p. 12.
193. *Learning and Living*, p. 43.
194. *Ibid.*, p. 45.
195. *Ibid.*, p. 47.
196. *Ibid.*, p. 21.
197. *Ibid.*, pp. 22–23.
198. *The Student and His Knowledge*, p. 51.
199. *Ibid.*, p. 50.
200. *Ibid.*, p. 53.
201. *Ibid.*, pp. 53–54.
202. *Ibid.*, p. 57.
203. *Ibid.*, p. 53.
204. *Ibid.*
205. *Ibid.*
206. *Ibid.*, pp. 55–56.
207. *Ibid.*, p. 56.
208. *Ibid.*, p. 68.
209. *Ibid.*
210. *The Papers of Christian Gauss*. New York: Random House, 1957, p. 294.
211. *The Quality of the Educational Process in the United States and in Europe*, p. 120.
212. *Ibid.*
213. *Ibid.*, p. 121.
214. *The Student and His Knowledge*, p. 58.
215. *Ibid.*, p. 59.
216. *Ibid.*
217. *The Future of the Liberal College*, preface.
218. *Ibid.*, pp. 22–31.
219. *Ibid.*, p. 31.
220. *Ibid.*
221. New York: McGraw-Hill Book Company, 1959, p. 140.
222. *The Quality of the Educational Process in the United States and in Europe*, p. viii.
223. *The American High School Today*, p. 15.

224. *The Quality of the Educational Process in the United States and in Europe,* p. 35.
225. *Ibid.,* p. 36.
226. *Ibid.*
227. *Ibid.*
228. *Ibid.,* p. 37.
229. *Ibid.,* p. 47.
230. *Ibid.,* p. 105.
231. *An Experiment in Responsible Learning,* p. 10.
232. *Ibid.*
233. *Ibid.*
234. *The Student and His Knowledge,* p. 50.
235. *Realism in American Education,* pp. 62–65.
236. *An Experiment in Responsible Learning,* p. 6.
237. *Realism in American Education,* p. 34.
238. *Ibid.,* pp. 34–35.
239. New York: Harper & Brothers, 1959, p. 127.
240. *Ibid.,* p. 89.
241. *New York Times,* May 24, 1959, p. 74.
242. *How Sputniks Made America Rethink Education: A Content Analysis of The Wall Street Journal.* Rollins College: Center for Practical Politics, 1958.
243. *Realism in American Education,* p. 35.
244. Personal letter dated June 1, 1959.
245. Edward D. Eddy, *The College Influence on Student Character.* Washington: American Council on Education, 1959, p. 185.
246. *Ibid.,* p. 9.
247. *Ibid.,* p. 10.
248. *Ibid.,* pp. 38–39.
249. *Ibid.,* p. 138.
250. *Ibid.,* p. 176.
251. *Ibid.,* pp. 179–180.
252. *Ibid.,* p. 177.
253. *Realism in American Education,* p. 13.
254. *Ibid.,* p. 70.
255. *An American Teacher's Year in a Prussian Gymnasium,* p. 370.
256. *The Quality of the Educational Process,* p. 4.

Bibliography

1911 *An American Teacher's Year in a Prussian Gymnasium:* A report to the Carnegie Foundation for the Advancement of Teaching. Reprinted from the Educational Record, April 1911. Pp. 345–370.

1914 *The Oberlehrer:* A Study of the Social and Professional Evolution of the German Schoolmaster. Cambridge: Harvard University Press. P. 150.

1920 *The Professional Preparation of Teachers for American Public Schools.* New York: The Carnegie Foundation for the Advancement of Teaching (Bulletin 14). P. 475.

1922 *Education in the Maritime Provinces of Canada.* New York: The Carnegie Foundation for the Advancement of Teaching (Bulletin 16). P. 150.

1924 *The American Public Library and the Diffusion of Knowledge.* New York: Harcourt, Brace & Co. P. 89.

1927 *The Quality of the Educational Process in the United States and in Europe.* New York: The Carnegie Foundation for the Advancement of Teaching (Bulletin 20). P. 133.

1930 *The College and the Freshman.* New York: The Carnegie Foundation for the Advancement of Teaching. Progress Report II, Study of the Relations of Secondary and Higher Education in Pennsylvania. P. 48.

1931 *Study of the Relations of Secondary and Higher Education in Pennsylvania.* New York: The Carnegie Foundation for the Advancement of Teaching. Progress Report III. P. 20.

1932 *Realism in American Education.* Cambridge: Harvard University Press (The Inglis Lecture). P. 70.

1933 *Admission to College.* New York: The Carnegie Foundation for the Advancement of Teaching. Pp. 23–48. (Reprinted by the foundation from *The Educational Record*—January 1933

1938 *The Student and His Knowledge*. New York: The Carnegie Foundation for the Advancement of Teaching. (Bulletin 29) Pp. i–xx; 406.

1940 *An Experiment in Responsible Learning*. New York: The Carnegie Foundation for the Advancement of Teaching (Bulletin 31). P. 61.

1941 *The Graduate Record Examination*. New York: The Carnegie Foundation for the Advancement of Teaching. P. 38.

1942 *What's in a Mark?* Reprinted from the Thirty-Seventh Annual Report (1941–1942) of the Carnegie Foundation for the Advancement of Teaching. P. 36.

1943 *Two Decades of an Educational Inquiry*. Reprinted from the Thirty-Seventh Annual Report (1941–1942) of the Carnegie Foundation for the Advancement of Teaching. P. 36.

Index